David A. Schulz is Assistant Professor of Sociology at The Pennsylvania State University. He is also an Episcopal priest, and a former consultant to the Church's urban pilot program. He has recently published an article on the role of the black lower-class father in *Sociological Quarterly*.

COMING UP BLACK

Patterns of Ghetto Socialization

David A. Schulz

Prentice-Hall, Inc. 

Englewood Cliffs, N. J.

To Helené and Lisa

 Library of Congress Catalog Card Number 69-15340. Printed in the United States of America.

Current printing (last number):
10 9 8 7 6 5 4

Prentice-Hall International, Inc. (*London*)

Preface

What is it like to grow up in a black ghetto? Despite the large and growing volume of books on poverty and the problems of black America, the life of the ghetto still remains something of an enigma to the average American. His distinctive style of life not only enables the ghetto dweller to cope more effectively with poverty and self degradation in the midst of an affluent and status-conscious society, it also makes it much easier for other Americans to avoid awareness of his pain and suffering—or if they become aware, to "write them off" as the just rewards of laziness or immorality. The time for such avoidance is running out.

The problems of the Negro family have come sharply into focus in the debate that centers around the Department of Labor's 1965 release, *The Negro Family: The Case for National Action.* The riots of that and the following summers have drawn further attention to the problems of the ghetto as America begins to realize that welfare and increased police protection are not enough "to keep the lid on the ghetto." Black poverty has bred black power and the demand that the nation take action to eliminate poverty, NOW!

This study attempts to overcome the middle-class myopia often experienced in looking at the ghetto by paying close attention to the process of growing up (coming up) in the ghetto of a mid-western city. The problems faced by children struggling to reach maturity here seem not too different from those faced by other children in New York, Washington or Los Angeles.

Particular attention is given to ten families—five complete and five broken—all of whom at one time lived in a large public housing project. The one hundred and eight persons who lived in these families were willing, over a three-and-one-half-year period, to "tell it like it is." The bulk of this study records their story in their words.

The author's interpretation of their account is, of course, subject to question and hopefully the criticism of further research. It bears inevitably the perspective of a middle-class American who can never really know, in the same way ghetto persons know, what it is like to be black and impoverished in America. Racism infests the whole of our society so completely that it can no longer be regarded as a peculiar pathology. It is a normal part of our way of life—something we take for granted. This too must be understood if one would understand the nation's black ghettos that exist not by accident or ill fortune, but by design. In looking at the problems of the ghetto, then, one sees but half the pattern.

I am in debt to many persons who have contributed to this study in various ways. This book is basically a revision of my doctoral dissertation, "Variation in Complete and Incomplete Families of the Negro Lower-Class" which I completed under Dr. Lee Rainwater by means of a grant from the National Institute of Mental Health (Grant No. MH-09189 "Social and Community Problems in Public Housing Areas"). Without his patience and constructive criticism, this study would not be. Several persons, who comprised the research team of which I was a member, also contributed to the ideas here expressed. In particular I wish to thank Dr. Alvin Gouldner, Dr. Jules Henry and Dr. David Pittman who were the principal investigators in the project and Dr. William Yancey, Mr. Boone Hammond, Dr. Jerome Stromberg, Miss Joyce Ladner, Miss Ethyl Sawyer and Mr. Robert Simpson, my colleagues. My indebtedness to these persons is more precisely indicated in the footnotes.

I would like to thank Dr. Howard E. Freeman for reading and commenting upon the completed manuscript and Dr. Neil J. Smelzer for his comments upon an earlier incomplete draft. Finally I thank Dr. Margaret Matson for her criticism and assistance in completing the manuscript and Miss Norma MacPherson for her diligent typing under the pressure of constant revision. The completion of the manuscript was made possible by a grant from The Pennsylvania State University (Grant No. 129).

Contents

Foreword

This book deals with a subject that has attracted considerable social science and public interest during the past few years as the nation has struggled to begin dealing with the northern, urban forms of its race problem. In connection with this struggle for understanding it may be of some interest to tell how David Schulz came to have an opportunity to carry out his research.

For generations the nation and its major cities have cared very little about the prospects and problems of the Negro Americans who make up a significant minority of their population. As time has gone on, however, and as the Negro populations have come to represent an ever larger proportion of those who live in central cities, governments and the establishments to which they are responsive have become increasingly concerned with doing something to resolve the problems of the slum ghetto. But this move to action has seldom been based on either genuine empathy for the people who live there or adequate understanding of the sources of their problems.

One public policy response derived from the very slight empathy and understanding the cities and the nation have of the Negro American situation has been the building of public housing projects. These projects were supposed to provide a better environment for the residents of the slums, as well as do away with the insult to city pride which unsightly slums represent. The City of St. Louis in the late 1940's responded to heightened awareness of its growing and deteriorating ghetto by planning a large, high-rise, segregated housing project to "help" some of the city's Negro citizens. The Captain Wendell O. Pruitt Homes and the William L. Igoe Apartments next to it were opened for occupancy in 1954. (The Igoe homes had originally been designed for segregated white occupancy, but the Supreme Court had ruled that unconstitutional, so both projects were theoretically to be integrated. In fact, in a very short time the population was almost exclusively Negro.)

Within a few years, however, the very real problems which continued to plague this ghetto community, despite its spanking new physical plant, augmented by heightened public sensitivity based on the frustrated expectations that somehow physical housing would make up for all that society had done to its tenants, resulted in the project's becoming as much of a problem as the slum which it was supposed to replace. The community and the federal government were appalled—Pruitt-Igoe had been meant to express the pride of St. Louis, instead it was becoming one of its shames. One of the many responses of the local and federal governments to the increasing consternation which events in the project caused was the funding of a major five-year research project to probe the social and community problems of this public housing area.

Thus, this particular intensive study of a small number of project families, along with the other studies by the research team, are part of the social science effort to inform society about itself. The findings of this and other studies, hopefully, will prove useful in avoiding the kinds of public policy errors which Pruitt-Igoe represents and will point the way toward alternative policies that truly improve the situation of the poor generally, and the Negro poor in particular.

David Schulz's study seeks to answer with richness of human detail the question of how poor migrant Negro families make a life for themselves in the cities, and how they make a home in which to rear their children—children who are often not wanted, but who once born must be loved and cared for. His study provides fresh insight into the ways these families prepare their children to live in the depriving and hostile world in which they are born.

Behavioral scientists have learned that most of the problems of those who live at the lower class level, and the problems that lower class people in turn make for the rest of the society, can be understood if conceptualized as a result of the lower class person's efforts to adapt to and cope with the relative deprivation of being so far removed from the average American standard. The people who are called poor and near poor live a life somewhat separated from that of the stable working-class and middle-class members of the society. The latter have generally been doing very well indeed in terms of material affluence; in many ways they have found their lives more and more gratifying as the country has progressed economically, even as the sense of alienation of the relatively most deprived has increased.

The lower class is defined by two tough facts of life as it is experienced from day to day and from birth to death. These are the facts of deprivation and of exclusions: the lower class is deprived because it is excluded from the ordinary run of average American working- and middle-class life, and it is excluded because it is deprived of the resources necessary to function in the institutions of the mainstream of American life (which is after all working-, and not middle-, class). The most basic deprivation is of course the lack of an adequate family income, but from this deprivation flows the sense so characteristic of lower-class groups of not having the price of admission to participation in the many different kinds of rewards that ordinary society offers, some of which cost money, but also a good many others (education, for example) that do not.

But, deprivation and exclusion are only the beginning of the troubles of the Negro lower class, and sometimes in day-to-day life they do not really loom largest as barriers to a sense of reasonable satisfaction and security about who and where one is. The economic system and the system of social segregation operate to concentrate Negro lower-class people into particular communities. In those communities, by virtue of their own troubles and by virtue of the indifference and exploitative attitudes of the rest of the society, there grows up a system of institutionalized pathology (to use Kenneth Clark's phrase) which characterizes ghettos and slum neighborhoods. It is this world, more than the objective facts of deprivation and exclusion *per se,* that impinges most directly on the Negro lower-class child as he grows up and on the Negro lower-class adult as he lives from day to day.

We are struck in reading Schulz's work by the ordinariness of life in Pruitt-Igoe, although some of the experiences of the people there may seem dramatic, pathological, or extreme. Life in Pruitt-Igoe, like human life anywhere, comes to take on a routine, taken-for-granted character as people develop adaptations which allow them to make it from day to day. It is the job of the social scientist to formulate the adapted ways of life which allow for routine living in what is a highly depriving and punishing world. Schulz's findings go a long way toward denying the romanticism some middle class Negro and white intellectuals engage in about the Negro family. We discover the pain and suffering of family living which is built into their daily lives. Though we may also see that out of that pain and suffering some Negroes create styles of art or black politics that middle-class observers can admire, studies such as this one make it difficult to forget the price that is paid for their creation.

Schulz's findings demonstrate most effectively the powerful forces which estrange family members and potential family members from each other in the ghetto. And, because the author is always concerned with what people do with their lives, rather than simply with the problems they have, we learn how, despite the estranging forces, men and women find, for shorter or longer periods of time, relationships that can be meaningful to them, though never secure or really comfortable. His typology of male marginality becomes a catalog of the ways men and women who would like to have stable, satisfying and conventional marital relations cope with the fact that such relationships are unavailable to them—the various types of boyfriend and husband roles represent different versions of the "next best thing."

In the process Schulz's findings highlight the central importance of a stable occupational status for men if aspirations for conventional marital forms are to be gratified. We see in the detailed case studies he presents the ways in which the occupational marginality of the men creates their marginality to their families.

And we see the effect on children as they catch on to the truth of the dead-endedness of their prospective lives; as they learn from their mothers and fathers, and mothers' boyfriends, and older brothers and sisters what kind of world they are to live in. They see that their futures are likely to be much the same as their parents' present. Then, being sensible human beings, they know they had best set about learning how to live within their world in such a way as to extract from it whatever gratifications it may offer.

It is studies such as this to which we must look for an understanding of ghetto life that can buttress strategies for social change based neither on excessive optimism (as in many of the current anti-war programs) or on hopelessness that the damage done by a "culture of poverty" is so pervasive that government programs can only ameliorate and not do away with poverty. Studies such as this, which show ghetto people coping with the exigencies of their lives in responsive and meaningful ways, though often ways strange and disagreeable to the rest of society, offer encouragement to policy makers on two grounds. First, by discovering those features of their situation to which ghetto styles are a response—principally economic marginality—the policy maker knows what to take as his main target. Second, by coming to understand that ghetto dwellers are not automatons of the dead hand of the past in the form of a poverty culture, the policy maker can know that if his policies seriously address the major forces constraining the ghetto dweller, he in turn will respond by adapting his behavior constructively to the new, improved situation.

October, 1968

LEE RAINWATER
Washington University

Chapter 1

A World of Trouble

Understanding the ghetto is a necessity of our time. The war on poverty, the riots, the civil rights movement, and now Black Power have caused America to look at the problems of this black "other America." We have not looked very deeply, but are, nevertheless, troubled by what we see.

Part of our problem is a matter of perspective. We don't know what it is like to live in a ghetto. Most people find it difficult to see beyond their own sense of propriety and discover the strengths and the weaknesses in another's way of life. Even social scientists often do not adequately interpret the ghetto to the larger public. They analyze it in terms of broad generalizations that do not do justice to the variations in life style found in even a small number of ghetto families. Large scale systemic analyses are indispensable to any attempt to overcome the problems of the ghetto, but they tend to lose sight of the human dimension. Identification with the plight of ghetto dwellers is thus made more difficult by the very attempts to understand it.

In this study ten families containing one hundred and eight persons "tell it like it is." [1] The analysis of their story focuses upon certain pat-

[1] The major criterion for selecting these families was that five be complete families and five be incomplete. In addition, the heads of households were to be under sixty and over thirty years old and to have at least some children in school. These families cannot be said to be representative in any statistical sense of the project population. Indeed, the study was undertaken with the conviction that not enough was known about these families to decide what the important variables were that might make a representative sample possible. Not all the variation in family life can be found in these ten families, but they represent the most common types of families and their styles of life are representative (in pattern if not proportion) of project life.

Some 250 ten hour days were spent interacting with members of these families over a three-and-one-half-year period from 1963 to 1967. The major techniques employed to study them were participant observation and open-ended interview-

terned responses to their problems, particularly those connected with growing up ("coming up") and forming a family.

All of these families at one time lived in a large housing project in a midwestern city.[2] Their project is well known in their metropolitan community. Its problems have been dramatically presented on television and in the newspaper, but few persons who do not live there go there.

THE PROJECT AND ITS IMAGE

The thirty-three eleven-story buildings of the "project" stand out sharply against the black deteriorating buildings across the street. When they were built in the mid-fifties, they were thought to be a "new standard of housing design" and were expected to "save not only people, but money." Built before the Fair Housing Laws made segregation in public housing illegal, about a third of the buildings were for white tenants and the remainder for black.

Now, even after the passage of these laws, the project is segregated in fact. The last white family—a Mennonite missionary's—left in the summer of 1963. Since then the only white occupants are researchers or summer service groups who come to live on a temporary basis. Women and children, living largely in broken families that are "on welfare," are the largest group in the project population, the next being large complete families where the father (because he is disabled and unemployable) is able to live with his family while they receive ADC. Small families with both parents still living together avoid the project as long as they can. Even when they have to live there a while, they move out as soon as they can.[3]

---

ing. In addition to these ten families which form the core of this study, information was gathered on eight other families that were less well known.

Finally, since this study was but a part of a much larger study of community problems, information collected by a staff of ten field researchers and four faculty advisors was available. This included two sample surveys conducted in the summers of 1965 and 1966. During the course of one of these, the author personally collected data on forty additional families.

[2] The names of all persons are, of course, pseudonyms. Certain aspects of their mode of living (such as jobs, peculiar disabilities, etc.) have also been altered to protect their anonymity.

[3] Data collected from the Housing Authority files indicate that in 1965 the

The project has a very bad press image. It means "vertical slum" to all who know about it. In the major daily newspaper an article tells about the hazards of fire-fighting in the project. ". . . One man has to stay with the fire equipment while the others go inside to fight the fires. . . . If a man doesn't stay with the equipment as a watchman, all the brass fittings are stolen by the time the fire is out. The thieves sell them for junk." In another article the director of the project is quoted: "The corridors have come to be known as 'the gauntlet.' . . . Tenants are likely to find themselves in the midst of a ball game, a fight or the object of obscene remarks as they walk through them." In yet another issue a full-page spread in the feature section punctuates its color pictures with the following remarks:

> The image of the project is one of crime, vandalism and anti-social behavior. The vacancy rate is high—about 26% [in October of 1965] because eligible renters are afraid to move in or wish to avoid the stigma of "project" living. The buildings themselves are formidable, rising above the surrounding slums like huge fortresses. The lawns are trampled and littered with glass. Inside, the corridor walls are unpainted and scrawl-covered, giving the impression of age and decay. The undersize elevators (which stop only at the fourth, seventh, and tenth floors) are brutally defaced, battered and reek of abuse. Unused laundry rooms and stairways, with light fixtures shattered, provide dark havens for illicit activities.

In this "fortress" live 10,736 persons including 7,532 youths under the age of twenty-one, 2,223 adult females, and "only" 990 adult males.[4]

---

average number of adults (persons over twenty-one) is 1.53 per household and that 53 per cent of the households have only one adult. In less than 2 per cent, this is a male. Forty-four per cent have two adults, and 3 per cent have three or more. The average number of minors in the households that have minors is 4.28 and the average number of persons, 5.57. Thirty-one per cent of the households have seven or more persons living in them, and 25 per cent have three or fewer. The modal age of the heads of households falls between thirty and thirty-nine years of age. These data are drawn from a sample of about 1700 households taken in 1965. The sample excludes those with a head of household over sixty and no minors present. See Jerome Stromberg, "A Preliminary Report on Housing and Community Experiences of (Project) Residents" (St. Louis: Washington University, Social Science Institute, Occasional Paper Number One, 1966), pp. 3–14, for a more complete breakdown of the project population.

[4] These figures are for October 1965. In 1960, however, Housing Authority data indicated that 1,789 persons lived in the project, 68 per cent of whom were under the age of twenty.

They are poor by almost any definition of poverty.[5] In addition, many are "disreputable" or "undeserving" because they "won't work" or "keep a man" or have children "outside of wedlock" or because they are thought to enjoy living in filth.[6]

The people of the project are not unaware of their bad press image. They are not unaware of their "undesirability" in the eyes of the general public. Some of them have internalized this image and think of themselves as "loose" people or, less negatively, simply not like "the man."[7] They are also not oblivious to the dangers that are very apparent in their immediate environment. They will tell you the elevators are dangerous. During the years 1963–66 several persons, adults and children, fell down the shaft when the door opened and no car was at the landing. The elevators are also the scene of holdups, muggings, and rapes. "People use the elevators and the halls to go to the bathroom," they complain. The odor is often so offensive that many prefer to use the stairs rather than apologize to an outsider who has to step over sizeable puddles. Women frequently note, "A woman isn't safe in the halls"; "the laundry rooms aren't safe, clothes get stolen and people get attacked." These are among the things considered "big problems" by tenants—common and concrete expressions of what they mean when they say that they live in a "world of trouble."[8]

However, the harshness and terror of this world of trouble must be balanced against the life that has been forged in the midst of it. This life has its joys and pleasures and presents an attractive face to the public—at least enough to make it possible for some to be able to romanticize about poverty. But with careful listening one becomes suspicious of the laughter of the ghetto. So much apparent gaiety has a purpose all too often in the zero-sum contest system of interpersonal

[5] The median family income in 1965 was $2,780, with 54 per cent of all families under $3,000.

[6] David Matza suggests that a significant number of the poor have an additional handicap to overcome in that they are labeled "disreputable" by the core society, and are thus forced into a cycle of enduring pauperization. They are the most "hard to reach" portion of the "other America." David Matza, "Poverty and Disrepute," in *Contemporary Social Problems*, eds. Merton and Nesbit (New York: Harcourt, Brace & World, Inc., 1966).

[7] In 1965 few made a virtue of being black. There were simply too many negative associations with blackness.

[8] As inferred from a randomly selected sample of 239 individuals representing 182 households in the project, on the basis of interview data obtained during the summer of 1965.

manipulation for personal satisfaction and gain.[9] Whatever carefree release can be found is eagerly embraced in front of a backdrop of misery from which it can never be dissociated.

Nevertheless, despite the hardships of their physical and social environment these families are not so "disorganized" that there is no order or warmth in their lives.[10] They are not so "deprived" that their homes are barren and their speech lacking in richness and humor.[11] They are not so "hard to reach" that they have lost touch with the world outside. Finally, their many problems may in part reflect the fact that they are served by single-purpose agencies.[12]

Television is a major means of linking project dwellers to the world outside. Ghetto walls are real enough to maximize the effect of exposure to this unreal world of conspicuous consumption and repetitiously real personal problems which are channeled into the living rooms of the project. Tenants watch TV all day long. They are tantalized and mesmerized by what they see. Television is not, however, all allure and deception. It can open up new insights, sometimes inadvertently—as during that week of unbelievable horror in November of 1963 when the assassination of a president was followed by the public "execution" of his presumed slayer, and the project awoke to the fact that white America was not basically different from the violence of their ghetto streets.

Most often they see the contrast between the affluence that is portrayed and the poverty that is so real surrounding them. It is this contrast that makes their poverty so "grinding." It is this contrast be-

[9] Lee Rainwater suggests that the expressiveness characteristic of ghetto life is part of a manipulative life style designed to extract maximum personal benefit from interpersonal interaction. "Crucible of Identity: The Lower-Class Negro Family," *Daedalus,* XCV (Winter, 1966), pp. 172–216. Boone Hammond, "The Contest System: A Survival Technique" (St. Louis: Washington University Essay Series in Sociology, December, 1965), develops the theme in terms of a "contest system."

[10] Albert Cohen, "The Study of Social Disorganization and Deviant Behavior," in Merton and Nesbit, *op. cit.,* suggests that the term "disorganization" has become so heavily value ladened as to be useless as a scientific concept.

[11] As many persons have observed, the language of the street is rich and the verbal interaction requires quick wit and a ready imagination. Ghetto persons, contrary to the findings of written tests of verbal skill, are far from lacking in these qualities. They must simply be measured verbally.

[12] See Arthur Shostak, "The Poverty of Welfare in America," in *New Perspective on Poverty,* eds. Shostak and Gomberg (Englewood Cliffs, N.J.: Prentice-Hall, Inc., 1965), for a brief critique.

tween their way of life and the taken-for-granted respectability of white middle-class America that makes their style of life so unrespectable.

The "walls" of the ghetto separating those living outside from those within the project are not merely external—a street marking the boundry between respectability and disrepute. They are erected inside the men who look across these boundaries; they prevent each side from seeing the other clearly.

FAMILY TROUBLES

In order to better understand the process of coming up in the ghetto, it is, therefore, necessary to consider first some of the more pressing problems confronting these ten families. Their basic socio-economic characteristics are given in Table I.

Overcoming a Rural Past

Although half of the families have lived in the city since the parents married, ten of the fifteen parents grew up in the rural South. Some of the families reflect this rural upbringing more than others. The Fraziers have lived in the city over ten years, yet reflect this rural background most. Having been "put in their places" so long in the South, they look with suspicion and a warped kind of admiration upon all whites. Lester (thirty-seven) tells of numerous instances where he has been swindled by white men for whom he has worked since he and his wife came North. They left the South because the white man Lester worked for would promise him a wage and pay him only enough to buy food, keeping him constantly in debt. They had hoped that things would be otherwise in the North, but with no formal education (both are illiterate), they must depend on their oldest boy, Richard (fifteen), to manage their affairs. They are suspicious of everyone and afraid of the city. Aside from kin who came before them, they have made few personal contacts in the city and feel very much alone in its midst.

They are also less able to influence it than most. Were it not for Richard, they would not even be able to deal with the bureaucratic institutions of the city. He handles welfare checks, government and housing notices, letters from teachers, and a host of other documents.

Table I BASIC SOCIO-ECONOMIC CHARACTERISTICS

Name of Family	*Size of Family*					*Size of Household, 1966*							*Ages*				*Income in 1966*							Estimated Income	Income in Housing Authority Files
	Total Family	Adults	Legitimate Children	Born Before Marriage	Outsiders	Adults	Children	Outsiders	In-Laws	Grandchildren	Boyfriend	Total Household	Father	Mother	Oldest Child	Youngest Child	Wages/Month	ADC/Month	Disability, V.A., etc.	Boyfriend/Month	Other/Month	Total Monthly	Income/Person/Year		
Buchanan	13	2	9	1	1	2	12	—	1	3	—	18	55	49	18	1	160	325	75	—	—	560	448	6720	6226
Patterson	18	2	8	2	6	2	8	—	—	—	—	10	45	42	19	9	446	—	—	—	40	506	607	6072	3982
Washington	14	2	10	2	—	2	6	—	—	—	—	8	51	47	19	13	364	—	—	—	?	364	546	4370	4370
Frazier	13	2	9	—	2	2	9	—	—	—	—	11	37	40	15	2	75	258	75	—	—	408	444	4896	—
Billit	7	2	1	1	3	2	2	1	—	—	—	5	44	31	9	4	—	114	65	—	—	179	429	2148	2148
SUBTOTAL	65	10	37	6	12	10	37	1	1	3	0	52	44.6*	41.8*	16*	5.8*	—	—	—	—	—	403.4	494.9	4841*	—
Brown	9	1	5	—	1	1	5	—	—	—	—	8	—	40	16	6	40	156	68	60	—	324	486	3888	4276
Perry	6	1	4	—	1	1	3	—	—	—	1	4	—	34	15	8	75	107	—	80	—	262	786	3144	2428
Parvin	7	1	6	—	—	1	6	—	—	—	—	7	—	33	11	5	—	179	—	—	—	179	321	2148	—
Ward	8	1	4	—	3	1	1	3	—	—	—	5	—	50	22	15	120	90	—	80	131	402	984	4824	—
Handy	11	1	9	1	—	1	10	—	—	—	—	11	—	33	17	3	—	225	—	120	200	545	592	6540	—
SUBTOTAL	41	5	28	1	5	5	25	3	0	0	1	35	—	38*	16.2	7.4	—	—	—	—	—	342.4	634	4108.8*	—
TOTALS	106	15	65	7	17	15	62	4	1	3	1	87	44.6	39.9	16.1	6.6	—	—	—	—	—	372*	564*	4475*	—

* Average

This responsibility earns him considerable status in the family. His parents resent this at the same time that they cannot do without his help. They wish that he would mind like he did when they lived down South, but Richard is the only member of the family who has become urbanized. He plays it cool, looks you over with the deceptive confidence of a man of the street, and wonders at his parents' fear of the city. He has moved five times with them because of this fear during the past year-and-a-half and is about ready to stop running.

The move to the city has thus made the generation gap in this family exceptionally great and reversed the usual allocation of power in significant ways.

While the Fraziers came to the city as a complete family, Dorothy Brown left the "boot heel" of southern Missouri with six of her eight children a little over seven years ago. Her father sharecropped a farm there and made at least an acceptable living for her and her five siblings. She came to the city without resources and with no knowledge of any kin who might be living in the city to whom she could turn for help. (Later she discovered that she had an uncle living in the city, but she never felt free to call upon him.) This unusually bold adventure was prompted by extreme disappointment with her second husband who had taken up with her best friend and then entreated her to let this friend come and live with them.

Dorothy prides herself on her ability to make the best of whatever comes her way. When she came to the city she went "on welfare" to supplement the meager $68.00 a month she received from her first husband's veteran's pension. A little over a year ago she decided to try it on her own and went to work doing odd jobs. Since then she has earned a living largely by her own resources.

Following the most common pattern, Ethyl Perry came to the city with her children about eight years ago knowing that two of her half-siblings lived in the city and could be depended upon for help. They stayed with their kin until they could find a suitable apartment of their own. Ethyl's half-sister lived in the project, and so Ethyl moved into an apartment in the building next door.

Whatever the reason for leaving the country, the city presents quite different problems. Even those with kin to help have a hard time adjusting. Most families only partially break with their rural past, returning annually to visit their country kin. The relative detachment from a large group of kinsmen, the faster pace of urban living, and the awakening of aspirations to live more comfortably and more productively—coupled with the realization that black people have a harder time than white earning a living in the city—make the transition from country to city a trying one.

Defining the Intimate Group

The detachment from kin that often occurs when families move to the city is coupled with other new pressures that are largely linked with the matter of earning a living. In the ghetto the persons one lives with, depends upon for support, bears children by, or seeks intimacy with are not so likely to be limited to those related by marriage or blood. So also, it does not follow that living with someone, calling upon them for support, or begetting children by them reflects the existence of an intimate relationship. The contingencies of life are such that households often contain persons unrelated by marriage or lineage who, nevertheless, are indispensable to the continued functioning of that household. Sometimes they may fit in well and be liked by everyone. At other times they may not. The question, then, of who is to be considered "in the family" is somewhat more open in the ghetto than in white middle-class America.

Ordinarily children born outside of wedlock ("outsiders") create such a problem. While they are found in both incomplete (female-headed) and complete types of families, they are more likely to be living with incomplete families. When the parents separate, the outside child, who may have been living with a maternal grandmother, is likely to move in with the mother. Since this occurs quite frequently when the outsider is in her teens, she immediately faces an authority problem with her half-siblings.

Mary Perry is one such outsider. She came to live with her mother and four half-siblings after her mother left her husband and moved to the city. Mary was fifteen and the oldest in the household.

> Since I am the oldest I think I should boss everybody in the house and they not going to give it to me. So I ask them nicely to give it to me, but it is up to me to take it. They get mad at me and start talking about my father . . . and sometimes we

> end up fighting between me and my brother. He gets mad 'cause I hit one of *his* sisters, he would say. And sometimes I get mad because he hit one of my sisters . . . I think if I had lived with my family, my brothers and sisters and their father, I think we all wouldn't be like we are now saying, "You're not my sister."

Camela Boiken (nine) is an outsider living with two younger half-siblings, her mother, and "stepfather." Her problems are not with her younger half-sisters, whom she takes care of with considerable skill, but with her "stepfather." He is jealous of the fact that she is smarter and more capable than his children. When they are in the same room he customarily ignores her—talking to her through her mother—or scolds her for not taking care of her younger half-siblings as she should.

Seventeen outsiders have been born to ten of the fifteen parents. Four are now living within the ten households.

Another type of person presenting a problem in defining the intimate group is the boyfriend. Terms such as "stepfather," "cousin," or "uncle" are often used to talk about a boyfriend to a person who is not well known by the family. This is particularly true in the project because of the Housing Authority rules prohibiting boyfriends from visiting in the apartments. But boyfriends are very much a part of family life in the project, nevertheless. Take, for example, the Perry family.

Scribbled on the door of the Perry apartment are pictures of the female anatomy in various attitudes of exposure likely to strike the middle-class soul as "obscene." Such drawings abound on the stairway walls of the project and, together with the many verbal ejaculations in lipstick and crayon, announce to all passers-by that sex is very much a central concern of those who live here. Nevertheless, the fact that such drawings are scribbled on the Perry's door and not on every other door in this stairway might suggest that it was of peculiar concern to those inside—at least as they are viewed by their neighbors, for these words and drawings were not put there by the Perry children. Further, a part of the conversation in the laundry rooms of the building in which the Perry's live concerns the extent to which Ethyl Perry has made herself available to men. This process of labeling is carried to its formal conclusion when she must sign the following statement on the back of her Application for Continued Occupancy: "I understand that if my daughter or myself have any more children born out of wedlock, I will have to move out of the project."

Ethyl resents the labeling and particularly the Housing Authority's attempt to restrict her access to boyfriends by officially prohibiting them from visiting her apartment.

> Well I don't think that's real fair 'cause first thing I don't think they means anything. Lots of them don't do anything but get a kiss *'specially if you are able to work* and I don't think that's fair.

She is happy to report, however, that not all social workers uphold the rules. In fact, all of the five incomplete families are visited by boyfriends, so it would seem that the rule is enforced infrequently.

Boyfriends are indispensable. Ethyl remarks:

> When I get through paying the house rent and two or three bills —insurance maybe—I don't have enough money left for food. . . . My friend buys my groceries every week and things like that. And if I need any extra money, I ask him for it and he'll give it to me.

The style of life reflected in the furnishings of the Perry apartment and the newness of the children's clothes testify to Ethyl's skillful manipulation of a series of boyfriends, one of whom bought over half her furniture in addition to her weekly food.

The reason why a boyfriend is essential to the life of the Perry household can be seen by considering their budget. When Ethyl moved into the project with her four children, she was receiving $133.00 a month ADC and paid $51.00 a month rent for a three bedroom apartment. This left her $82.00 a month with which to feed, clothe, and in other less obvious ways support a family of five. Since she is very anemic and is usually in poor health during much of the year, she did not work at first. Now that she works, her wages as a part-time domestic add $72.50 a month to her ADC check, giving her a monthly income of $192.20. (Her yearly income is not simply twelve times this amount because she cannot depend upon the $72.50 every month.) Her rent is now $66.00 a month and that leaves $126.20 on which to live. From this she puts aside $5.00 a month as an "allowance" for each child. Few would argue that $101.20 is enough money to support a family of five. Ethyl sighs, "I'm happy enough, I guess. I got kids. I got a good home. Course I always look forward to finding me a good man."

Raymond, the last and current in her series of boyfriends, in contrast to his predecessors has moved into the Perry apartment and has succeeded in turning Ethyl's mind toward getting a divorce from her husband. This, more than anything else, has convinced her children that she is serious about Raymond.

Finally, several other factors operate to extend kinship terminology to a number of non-kin persons, thereby contributing to the problem of defining the intimate group. The first of these is the custom of "farming out" children to kin or close friends. These persons are ordinarily addressed by the child as "mother" or "father," even though it is known that biologically this is not the case. Children who are thus farmed out may return later in their lives to live with their real parents but continue to visit the "adopted" parents regularly. Such children may also experience difficulty relating to their siblings when they return.

The frequent occurrence of children born outside of wedlock contributes to the extension of the kinship terminology to non-kin persons. Families will sometimes consider themselves related to each other by this event even though no marriage occurs or is actively sought. The event of the child's birth seems to provide enough of an occasion to cement relations between otherwise unrelated families. This suggests the importance of the kinship bond in an environment where friends and neighbors are not easily called upon for assistance.

A third factor fostering the use of kinship terminology is identification as a member of a black brotherhood; although common now, however, this factor was not prevalent in the project during the period 1963–1967. "Member" still sufficed to indicate this relationship with a fellow black. Now "brother" and "sister" are used and have much more emotional significance than when they were used to hail fellow members of a church congregation.

Because the lower-class Negro family is so impoverished, they find it necessary to insure a ready supply of persons who can be depended upon when a crisis occurs. The extension of the intimate community—in name if not always in depth of relationship—serves to enhance the likelihood of a ready supply of such persons. At the same time, these relationships are not as dependable as they might be if these persons were in fact related. The expression of intimacy through the dimension of "caring" (economically, emotionally) is uncertain. One is more likely in the ghetto to share bed and board with another upon whom one is dependent and for whom one feels little affection. So likewise the circle of one's intimates is more likely to include well loved adults who are not able to provide for one's family when kinship dictates that they should.

Obtaining Adequate Housing

Another persistent problem of ghetto families is that of finding adequate housing. The project was built to meet that need, but it has not met even the needs of these ten families. Four have moved out—two, the Wards and the Handys, were evicted; and two, the Parvins and the Fraziers, left voluntarily.

The ghetto surrounding the project extends across the north central portion of the city. While at one time major streets, parks, or railroads marked its precise boundary, now zones of transition are more characteristic. Migration at present is northward and westward. The project is in the east central section, and so much of the inner-city migration is away from it. This tends to heighten its sense of undesirability.

The neighborhood immediately surrounding the project offers for the most part delapidated buildings with substandard or completely nonfunctional plumbing and heating facilities. While a three room "shotgun apartment" can be rented for around $35.00 a month plus utilities, it is not uncommon for the poor to pay more for their living space than the working or middle-class person and to receive much less.

Tilly Handy and her ten children were evicted from her mother's (Mrs. Buchanan's) apartment in the project because the Buchanan's five room apartment was grossly overcrowded—the Buchanans are a family of eighteen. Tilly now lives about three blocks from her mother's apartment. One or the other of her two oldest boys live with their grandmother, and Tilly and her pre-school children visit the Buchanans almost daily. There is a "For Sale" sign in front of the Handy apartment. When the people downstairs moved out, Tilly moved downstairs. They stayed in this building because it was close to the project, even though they knew they might have to move again soon.

Like most of the buildings in the neighborhood around the project, the building in which the Handys live was built in the last century. In the Department of Commerce census tract, 59 per cent of the dwelling units are classified as deteriorating, 65 per cent as deteriorating and dilapitated.[13] The yards are littered with glass, broken down automobiles, and an ever increasing accumulation of paper blown from the street. Adjacent to their back yard a neighbor toils at reclaiming lumber from the tumbling down buildings. His accumulation of building material fills his back yard and overflows into an empty lot.

Inside the house where the Handys live the hall is quite dark. The only light comes from an exposed light bulb on the second floor and is insufficient to penetrate the gloom of the first floor. The eyes must become accustomed to the dark to discover the crumbling plaster walls and the ancient wallpaper barely clinging to the more resistant plaster. The Handys prefer this house to the project, however, because they feel more "on their own" here.

Lilly Parvin and her six children left the project because Lilly found the tenants unfriendly and felt that she could not adequately take care of her children from the tenth floor apartment assigned to her by the Authority. She now lives in a three room roach infested apartment two blocks north of the project. The toilet upstairs overflows into her kitchen and she is afraid to open the basement door because of the enormous number of insect squatters. The apartment is much worse than Lilly had hoped, but it is on the ground floor, there is a small yard in the rear, and (in view of her own illness) it is about the best that she could do.

Both the Wards and the Fraziers have moved several times since leaving the project. After three moves over a two-year period, the Wards now reside in the western portion of the ghetto, but face another move soon because their apartment building has been bought by an oil company for a service station. The Fraziers have moved five times in the little over a year since they left the project the first time. They tried to live in the project twice since they first left, but each time found the environment too "tough" for them. Their last stay

[13] U.S. Department of Commerce, Bureau of the Census, *City Blocks,* 1960.

lasted only three days. Mae Apple was roughed up and robbed of her ADC check the month before Christmas. At first the Fraziers tried moving west, but found the rent too high. Now they live in a two story row house about five blocks east of the project. A large trucking company has its depot across the street.

Ghetto families move a lot, but the moves do not mean increasing status and a better way of life. At best their style of life remains essentially the same. At worst the tyranny of slumlords and the exploitation of newly found neighbors increase their burden of deprivation and expose them more completely to the violence of ghetto streets. Further, the constant moving creates an almost insurmountable problem for their school-age children, many of whom attend five or six schools before they get out of grade school. School progress is thus retarded and another generation locked more securely inside ghetto walls. Everywhere the accumulation of disadvantages works against ghetto dwellers to reduce their chances of escape.

Overcoming Deprivation

The Range of Deprivation

Income is only a partial measure of deprivation. The accumulation of the disadvantages of ghetto life seems most sharply portrayed in the Parvin family. When the Parvins lived in the project, they lived above the Wards, and after the Wards moved out, above the Perrys. The contrast between the Parvin apartment and the apartment below them in each case was quite apparent. The most characteristic feature of the Parvin household was its isolation and disorganization.

At thirty-three Lilly Parvin has been hospitalized for mental illness. Her illness in part prevents her from being able to benefit materially from her boyfriend's visits. She craves companionship but fears men. She even at times fears her eight-year-old son Jerry, whom she becomes convinced is spying on her. When her boyfriend comes to visit, he "rapes" her. He comes and goes as *he* pleases. The Parvin apartment is usually bleak and dirty. The hand prints of the six children (who are most often confined within the apartment because of Lilly's fear that they will be exposed to the wrong kind of children) create a dark messy stain all along the walls to a height of about four-and-a-half feet, the distance being higher above the sofa where the foothold permits further exploration.

When Lilly first came to the project after being expelled from her father's house by her "stepmother," she had but one bed, a dining room table, several dishes, an inadequate number of eating utensils, and a few cooking pots. These were all in the living room, where the whole family slept. The older children shivered on cardboard pallets on the exposed concrete floor, the younger three huddled close to their mother on the single bed. The second-hand clothes picked up at churches or the Salvation Army store lay in piles in the closet when not in use.

The furniture, which is provided periodically by Lilly's welfare worker, is always quickly destroyed by the loud destructive activity of the children, who seem to be playing on the edge of anger that now and then erupts into violent outbursts against siblings, and occasionally against their mother. In her illness Lilly fears all of her children, who seem to take advantage of the situation and taunt their mother.

Ironically, Lilly's illness brings her into more "contact" with her kin than do her daily activities. She sees visions of dead and living relatives and is haunted by her mother. She married because of a pregnancy while her mother was on her deathbed; now she fears that her mother still believes that she deserted her. An older sister tantalizes her. She would like to emulate this sister's feminine ways and her greater moral perfection, and would even have joined the Sanctified Church but for the fact that she considers herself too depraved to be saved. Her husband, from whom she has been separated since shortly after the birth of Richard, joins her visionary world. She believes that while she lived with him, he tried to work hoodoo on her and shrink her into a tiny doll. He taunts her by bringing his girlfriend into her visionary world. The characters of this visionary world are at times more real and threatening than her own rambunctious children.

This illness is most pronounced in Lilly, but it has also affected her children. Willie Mae (nine) was expelled from school and ordered to take a psychiatric examination because she would not talk to her teacher. Jerry is very aggressive, acting out his aggression in dramatic combat with unseen assailants. Richard, now five, has only begun to utter words. When he first came to the project he rarely made a sound.

He endured his continual colds in silence. By contrast, the older two daughters appear quite normal. They are the most dependable contact that the family has with the world outside its apartment. They shop, cook, and take care of all members of the household, including their mother when she is ill, even though Kim is only eleven and Stephanie ten.

Aside from infrequent baskets of food from kin, the family's sole source of income is Lilly's ADC check, which brings them $2,428 a year. Even though few families could live very well on this amount (in the city in 1966), the Parvin's deprivation is much more extreme. Lilly's illness has cut them off from the help of a boyfriend, and her father's stepmother has succeeded in separating her from her father's help. Thus, the Parvins have not been able to accumulate any significant amount of possessions. While the disorganization of this family is undoubtedly extreme, it is nevertheless representative (in pattern if not in proportion) of problems common in the project.

Somewhere near the other end of the scale of deprivation reflected in these ten project families are the Washingtons. The Washingtons came from the delta country of southern Missouri twenty-five years ago, and today they only occasionally show signs of their rural upbringing. This family of twelve has several older children who are married and living elsewhere. The household contains only eight, including Arthur (fifty-one) and his wife Lotta (forty-seven), and their six children ranging in age from thirteen to nineteen.

Their apartment boasts nearly new furniture that is carefully protected by plastic slipcovers. There is a prominent bar with the appropriate glassware for several kinds of cocktails separating the living room from the dining room area. This is a symbol of good living, of which the family is very proud. The large deepfreeze and new television also contribute to the image of affluence—but both of these have very important mundane roles to play in the daily routine, and therefore are not quite as significant as symbols of the good life.

For over nineteen years Arthur was the major wage-earner in the family. Gradually, as the size of his family increased, he took over additional jobs in the evening and his wife began to work part time. About three years ago, Arthur was laid off from his assembly line job and told by the employer that he would "get in touch when he needed him." Arthur branched out into the moving business and is able—with the help of a rapidly deteriorating pickup truck—to earn a little money. His wife now works full time as a domestic.

The Washingtons are friendly in a reserved sort of way. Although they were involved in this study for three-and-one-half years, comparatively little is known about them. This is in part because Arthur has increasingly resorted to illegitimate means to supplement his income and is therefore suspicious of all visitors. He and three of his sons have been arrested for gambling and Arthur has served a short term for possessing lottery equipment. The boys help their father in both his legal and illegitimate occupations.

Because Arthur's hours are much less regular than his wife's, he is able to assume the responsibility of keeping the house and preparing some of the evening meals so that Lotta will not have to do this when she comes home tired. His older daughters help him keep the house, but his sons find little to their liking in household chores. As a result of the efforts of all, however, the apartment is much more than simply a place to sleep. It is the center of the family's life and a safe place for children and grandchildren who come for help and comfort.

Excluding an unknown amount of money earned illegally, the family's income in 1966 was $6,072.

Mobility Means "Going It Alone"?

Because of the severe handicaps placed upon the adult males in earning a living, project families are not likely to be able to move out of poverty as a family. Individual members may succeed, and when they do they are generally praised by their families even though they can do little to help others in the family overcome poverty. Their own position is often quite marginal. Parents have many children and console themselves that in their old age the children will take care of them, but all too often the children are not around or, if they are, are unable to help their parents much more than their parents helped them.

In the case of these ten families, it does not seem likely that the parents ever will know any style of living much different from what they now experience. None of the older married children has done much better to date than his parents. They all live within the ghetto in inadequate housing, have less than a high school education, and poor paying jobs with no future. Those children now of high school age show somewhat more promise. Two boys and two girls have graduated from high school (a recent return visit in 1968 disclosed that one of the girls is college bound) and several others seem likely to graduate. However, both boys are married and have children. They have not as yet been able to find jobs that offer them either a decent wage or a reasonably dependable career with a chance to do better in the future. Unless they find such jobs their future in the ghetto looks bleak. The girls who have graduated are single and career oriented. Only the one bound for college, however, seems likely to find a mate who will be able to secure her a footing outside of poverty.

At present the journey out of poverty is an exceedingly difficult one, accomplished, if at all, ordinarily by lonely individuals who courageously go it alone. The help and good wishes of their families are as often as not countered by the hindrance of their social and economic environment both inside of the ghetto and out. Most teenagers dream of overcoming poverty but for many the realities of their present life have left them too deeply wounded to struggle upward; yet, when they give up and drink their days away they cannot, even then, forget their failure or put aside their dream.

Coming up in the ghetto is, therefore, a process quite infused with the yearning to overcome poverty and be free. For young and old such yearning is all too often a dream deferred until its promise fades in the melancholy reflections of old age. Children must learn effective means of coping with the problems of poverty without having this yearning for a better life dampened—even though such yearning makes living in the midst of deprivation more painful. That each generation learns anew both the means of surviving under the burden of such deprivation and the hope that in their time it can be overcome, is one of the wonders of the human spirit. It is, therefore, to a more detailed examination of the process of coming up in the ghetto that we now turn.

Chapter 2

Coming Up as a Girl in the Ghetto

Common themes in the conversation of the women of the project concern the problems and pleasures of raising children. Generally coming from large families and having large families of their own, the women are exposed to the problems of caring for young children for a considerable portion of their lives. This fact is often intensified, as in the case of the Buchanans, when their grandchildren come to live with them also.

By the age of nine a girl has already been given considerable responsibility over her younger siblings: washing them, changing their diapers, feeding them, and in general watching over their play. She is helped, however, by most other members of the family, particularly her sisters. Her care is not expected to extend to the babies, except perhaps for an occasional feeding if the mother is not breast feeding the infant (breast feeding is rare in the project). By thirteen she can "have the child." When the mother comes home from the hospital she quite often gives the baby to the oldest daughter within a few days and this daughter then sleeps with the baby and assumes responsibility for its daily welfare.

For these mothers conception as well as child care characteristically begins before marriage when they are in their teens. These aspects of maternity, therefore, come to constitute major components of what it means to be a "girl," and are not specifically linked to the role of wife-mother. The experience of these ten mothers in bearing and caring for children while they were coming up is, furthermore, an important factor in shaping the image of the feminine role for their daughters and directly influences the interaction that takes place between mother and child. The character of the home depends, then, in part upon this early experience.

Young Mothers

The mothers of these families began caring for children very early in life. They cared for their mother's children (a first-born daughter will not speak about these children as her "brothers" or "sisters," but will refer to them as "her" children) or baby-sat for neighbors or relatives who had to work in the fields. Some of them began to care for their own children before they were sixteen.

Most of their earliest experiences in caring for children came while they were living in the country. In the weather-beaten sharecropper's shanty called "home," life was slower, paced to the sun and seasons, and there was room to expand and play outside. As adults, they have had to raise most of their children under the quite different circumstances of the city. Older parents talk about the change the city has made:

> They say time brings a change. It just ain't like it used to be. I can tell by my children. I try to bring mine up like my mother brought us up. It's just a difference in children these days. I guess it's because they're in the city and we were in the country. Here they see everything and hear everything so everything is a different set up.
>
> (woman, age 47)

> I didn't know what courting was, not like these children here. Children these days got more than us when we was coming up. Grand Mama was tight on us. She wouldn't let us go nowhere.
>
> (woman, 40)

> I think that a city life is more or less the life that has ruined so many children . . . because they don't have anything to do. If he isn't in my backyard, he's in yours and if he's not there, he's in this other man's, and they just don't have room enough to get around so that they can play to themselves without interfering with somebody else.
>
> (man, 45—without a yard)

Their mothers fed them at the breast; they feed their babies with a bottle. In the country toddlers could crawl about outside without constant supervision. In the city, and particularly in the project, they cannot. They were raised in a rural community where the preacher warned against sinning and neighbors were church members. In the city most people do not go to church. All parents agree that children were better disciplined when they (the parents) were coming up.

It is difficult to document precisely the effect of this change in the larger context of child rearing when one had not been able to observe the "before situation." It is an important change, nevertheless, because what worked with children in the country community might not work in the city, and that presents a problem in adaptation which some mothers are able to handle more easily than others. For some mothers the problem of child care is further complicated by the fact that they have had greater responsibility in child rearing than many of their contemporaries. This exposure is, as one would expect, related to their birth order.

The First Born

Alliena Billit recalls her early experience in taking care of her siblings. In 1939, when she was three years old, her family (both parents and two siblings) moved from the South to Chicago. A baby brother, Harry, was born on the train and Alliena, being the oldest, had the task of helping to care for the child:

> Most of my recollection is looking after the baby. I remember mother carried me to a rocking chair to hold the baby. To keep the baby she'd tie me in the rocking chair and that's the way she would do her work.

Alliena's recollection of child care when she was coming up is almost totally enclosed in negativistic attitudes of the adults in her immediate environment and the harsh reality of poverty. Her mother was chided for having given birth to a child out of wedlock, and Alliena remembers the attitude of her grandfather, who complained that her mother had enough children—a point he never failed to make with the birth of each successive child. Part of the reason for the family moving from Mississippi to Chicago was her grandfather's scoldings.

In Chicago the family was very poor and their house was always cold in the winter:

> I remember Harry's teeth chattering and I got up to see what it was. I kept yelling "Jarvis, Jarvis, Jarvis, wake up!" You know how kids were. You hear a noise and you don't know what it is. So we peeped out from under the cover and I saw Harry up in the bed. He had wet on himself. So I took his diaper off of him and got him off the cot and put him on the floor with us up under all these blankets. And I can remember mama running from the kitchen up to this little room we had saying, "Where's my baby? Where's my baby?" . . . And I woke up and said, "Well Harry is on the pallet." She said, "Oh you'll kill him, you'll kill him!" And from then on I started taking care of . . . *her babies*. . . . I washed diapers and fix bottles and kept them clean. *Just a baby sitter. I just took care of the kids.*

At the time there was a mixture of pride and anger in this appointed task—pride in that she was the only one who was trusted to care for her siblings (and was thus demonstrably older and wiser than any of them), anger at the imposed responsibility that deprived her of her freedom. She expressed her negative feelings about the birth of one of her siblings in a letter to a friend. The letter came back because it had no stamp on it and her mother opened it and read, "I hope this little brat dies." Alliena remembers her mother's punishment:

> She read it. She wanted to know how I knew she was pregnant. I said, "Didn't you tell me?" She said, "Naw, I didn't tell you 'cause I didn't know myself. So you don't want to have nothing to do with this brat?" So [after that] everything I did wrong she'd rub that in. I'd tell her, "Aw God, I was just saying that because I was mad." It looked like most of the time when I got ready to do something she'd say, "You've got to do so and so." And then she would explain to me why I didn't have time to do things like other kids. Anyway, when Mary was born she looked like a little hairy ape. . . . She wouldn't let me take care of the baby. She said, "Ann, here, you can have this baby." And I couldn't touch the baby. I would get up to fix the baby's bottle and she'd say, "I didn't tell you to do it. Put it down." That would hurt me so bad.

Thus, Alliena grew up to resent "kids" even though her mother tried to console her from time to time with the thought, "There's nothing wrong with numbers." Despite her punishment of not being permitted to care for the last two babies, she nevertheless was the one that most often disciplined her siblings:

> I remember when I would whip the kids she would tell me, "Alliena, I don't mind you whipping the kids because you have to take care of them and I know you can't make them mind without whipping them, but don't beat nare one of *my* kids." I said, "I don't beat them I whip them." She said, "You beat *my* kids and I don't want you doing that."

At several crucial times in her life, both her mother and father deserted the family and Alliena was solely responsible for her siblings. This constant responsibility has had its effect. When she entered the local teacher's college at her mother's insistence, she was very ambivalent about working with children, stating that she didn't feel that she had the patience to work with them. She flatly states that she did not want children. Nevertheless, her first child was born out of wedlock when she was twenty-two and her second conceived out of wedlock at twenty-five. All of her three pregnancies were very painful and the last nearly cost her her life. The last child, Louise (four), squeals and cries but does not talk. She is cared for to a great extent by Alliena's oldest girl, Camella (nine), a very dependable and capable housekeeper.

Dorothy Brown (forty) was born in the "boot-heel" of Missouri but, because of her very poor health coming up, was not able to work the fields. She took care of the children. Now she complains:

> I'm overrun with children all the day long. . . . I don't care how I holler. They are here. . . . I just seem to attract them, it seems ever since I was seven years old. . . . My mother, when she started to working, I started taking care of the kids, even when I was little. . . . When anybody would go to work, they knowed I was staying home and they would drop them by our cabin and leave them. I've been catching children ever since. . . . [It] don't bother me. I love children.

Dorothy had the responsibility of caring for five siblings, the major portion of the wash around the house, and cooking the evening meals on occasion. She was, like Alliena, the oldest child. Her first child, Ann, was born outside of wedlock when she was seventeen; her second, Delores, "outside" at twenty-four. She married when she was twenty-five and has given birth to a total of eight children, three of whom are outsiders.

While she baby-sits for extra money and claims that she "loves children," she is not sure of herself with them. She also fears that she will lose her patience and beat them:

> The most problems with me and the children is when I tell them to quit doing something and they just keep on. Then I gets nervous and at the same time I'm scared to hit them. I'm scared I might hit them too hard, because on the 21st of this month, which will be three years ago when I was in the hospital operated for a broken vein, the doctor told me that when them spells hit me and the children get me so bad, and my nerves are so bad, I should try to grab myself and not hit them, because I might go a little bit too far.

Tilly Handy (thirty-three) was born "outside" when her mother was only fourteen. She conceived her first child at the age of barely fifteen, making her mother a grandmother at the age of twenty-eight. She and her mother were both pregnant about the same time, both conceiving their second child in the same year, one month apart. She was seventeen, her mother thirty-one. However, by the time she had her third child, Mark, her mother had had four children, with a fifth to come three months later. Thus, when Tilly left her first husband and returned to live with her mother, she brought with her three children, ages one through six, and her mother had six children within the same age span. Tilly had to watch over nine childen under six before she was twenty-one:

> All the kids and us got along fine. I would buy clothes for *her kids,* and she would buy for mine. When she would go out I would keep the kids. They was just like they was mine, 'cause I kept them. While they [the mother and "stepfather"] was at work I kept the kids. So they didn't have no problem; they could work and stay on the place.

She and her mother have always reared their children together. Even when Tilly was married and living away from the Buchanans, the older children especially would come back to stay with their grandparents. In this overlapping of child rearing responsibility, the children have developed a rather interesting nomenclature. They call their maternal grandfather "pa pa," their maternal grandmother "mother," and their mother "Tilly." Despite the work Tilly may or may not have done in contributing to their upbringing, the Buchanans retain a place of priority in the lives of her children and are perceived as a locus of stability.

Lotta Washington (forty-seven) is the first-born girl who was bothered least by her parents' children. She recalls the arrival of her brother when she was five:

> I was a small girl and I had to work in the field to gather the crops. I was very excited over my baby brother. . . . We were all excited.
>
> *Q:* Who took care of him?
>
> Well, my sister [who was four], the one next to me. I didn't have too much to do with the baby. She had patience. I liked the baby, but I couldn't just sit up and nurse babies. . . .
>
> *Q:* Did you ever care for a baby?
>
> Oh yeah, I cared for *her babies.* Cause she had [six] babies after this one . . . but just say nursing, I didn't. But I kept the baby. I would have to go to the field and pick cotton and help work in the field.

Thus Lotta's orientation from an early age was not as strongly in the direction of raising children, for the lot fell mainly on her sister. Lotta's first child died nine months after birth; in her next delivery she gave birth to twins, one of whom died. She has raised twelve children, beginning when she was sixteen and ending at the age of thirty-four (twelve children in eighteen years). This number was considerably larger than her early desires:

> Well I never did want but one child. I was young and I didn't realize, but *now* I'm proud of my family. I figure when you get old you should have children to help you. *Then* I just didn't want no bunch of children.

Those Born in the Middle

The recollections of these women are varied. In general, they did not have the same heavy responsibility placed on them as did the first-borns, and so their attitudes toward children are more benevolent.

Having been born "outside" as the result of an extramarital affair, Ethyl was reared in the family of her mother and her husband. She never did much caring for her siblings. Her closest sibling was her older half-sister Carol, also born to her mother "outside" but before marriage. Ethyl's double onus (being "outside" and "extramarital") set her apart. She continued in her mother's footsteps by conceiving a child, Mary, "outside" when she was fifteen. However, she married a man other than Mary's father before Mary was born. Six months after Mary's birth she was pregnant with her second child, James. Ethyl's experience in raising children has been largely limited to raising her own. Mary was taken off her hands shortly after she was born and raised by her maternal grandmother until she was fifteen, when she came to the city to join her mother and half-siblings. Ethyl bore four children to her husband, the first three at two-year intervals, the last after a period of five years. She gave birth to a total of five children over a period of ten years.

Mae Apple Frazier (forty) also was born "outside," but in the context of eight such children born to her parents. Her two older siblings are illegitimate and she has five half-siblings who never resided with her who also are illegitimate.[1] Mae Apple's home life was very broken, both parents "cutting out" on each other. She left home at the age of thirteen to live with a maternal aunt. Her recollections of her early childhood do not include the care of children, for she worked a great deal in the fields and later in the great house of the plantation. At the age of ten she replaced her mother, who then went reluctantly to work in the fields. Mae Apple bore her first child, Janie, "outside" when she was nineteen. Her child-bearing period extended from that age until thirty-nine, and during these twenty years she has given birth to nine legitimate children, her second child coming six years after her first, when she was twenty-five.

Mae Apple's affection for her children is more apparent than that of many of the mothers because she prefers to breast feed her infant, Stewart. Thus she is mainly responsible for him for a longer period of time than are mothers who prefer a bottle. While she suckles her

[1] The practice of common-law marriage is probably more common in Mae Apple's experience than in that of the rest of the women in the study, but she designates herself an "outsider," which most probably reflects a very unstable living relationship between her parents.

baby, her children watch with great admiration and affection. For Mae Apple babies are a pleasurable part of life, and one has the impression that she could bear many more children without losing her basic affection for them. Her major problem as a mother raising children in the city is her tendency to want to keep her children too close to her.

When Leona Wards (fifty) was ten, her mother died, and she and a brother and sister went to live with her maternal aunt. The couple never had children of their own, and so Leona and her siblings were most welcome. However, according to the strict interpretation of the "thou shalt not's" of the Baptist faith, they were made to "toe the line." Thus, what Leona remembers about her early childhood is not the care of children but the strict discipline she encountered while living with her aunt and uncle.

She married "as a virgin" when she was seventeen. Her older sister also married as a virgin. Leona raised four children by her husband, the first coming when she was eighteen, the last when she was twenty-eight. Two boys died in infancy, one from swallowing glass, the other from dropsy. This marriage lasted fourteen years, despite much turmoil and conflict between Leona and her husband. After a four-year pause, she bore three more children, all by the same boyfriend, Larry, ending her child bearing career at the age of thirty-four.

While she was growing up, Leona was not held responsible for any of her siblings because her aunt wanted to assume this prerogative; later her oldest daughter, Luemer (now thirty-two), took care of her own children. Leona gives the impression of having the warmest attitude toward children of any of the mothers thus far considered. More than most mothers, she reacts warmly with the small children in the project, who frequently knock on her door for candy. After giving them some she characteristically says, "Now you sugars come back."

Lilly Parvin (thirty-three) is mentally ill and was hospitalized for this illness for a period in 1967. Her recollection, therefore, is impaired, and what she brings to the surface about her childhood and her caring for children is obscure. She talks about her mother in general but will not provide details: "My mother was a Christian. My father was a pretty nice guy. [My home] was nice, nice surroundings and all that for that time." Lilly was the fourth oldest child, having one illegitimate half-sister and two sisters older than she.

Her inner conflict focuses around her strongly ambivalent feelings about her sisters, who are prettier than she and who, in two instances, have disgraced the family (in her opinion) by having outside children. She herself conceived her first child outside, but married the father and lived six years with him. She bore him five more children before he abandoned her. She is overwhelmed with guilt over her inability to live as a Sanctified person would. She is not a member of this denomination, but considers its teachings the most perfect law and herself unworthy of joining. Her sporadic, guilt-ridden lovemaking with a boyfriend has as yet produced no children. Once when she thought she was pregnant, she reported that she hoped she would have a boy, as she always wanted one. She seems oblivious of the fact that she already has three.

In summary, those fortunate enough to be born in the middle do not have embedded in their memory the drudgery of caring for children while coming up themselves. Most of them helped in baby-sitting and other chores, but none of them were "given a baby" to raise. The problems of being born in the middle stem from areas other than child care—sibling rivalry having perhaps the highest claim on the complaint list of these women. Three of the four women in this group are now separated from their husbands. Three of the four have also born children outside of wedlock. The only family evicted from the project because of the antisocial behavior of the children has a mother who is a middle child. Finally, the only female hospitalized for mental illness is a middle child. Whether these facts are related to the birth order of the mother is difficult to prove, but the problems of these households do seem more acute.

The Last Born

The last born have had the least exposure in caring for *her* (their mothers' children.

In addition to being the baby of her family, Della Mae was also a seven-month baby who was quite sickly through much of her childhood until she was in her middle teens:

> I mostly did the caring for the smaller children cause I was the only one at the house. My mother always left me at the house. During the time they had to do the work in the field and I did

> the housework and cared for the small children and tried to have the meals ready on time. I was cooking for the whole family.

Della Mae began this care when she was fifteen and continued it until she was twenty. Prior to that time she was more cared for than caring. One of the "smaller children" cared for was her own illegitimate first child, Dorothy, who was born to her when she was fifteen. The others were not in the main her own siblings but were neighbor or kin children brought to the cabin for baby-sitting while their parents worked in the fields.

Della Mae regards her family home as a happy one where everyone talked things over. Her major recollection of childhood is not in terms of the work she did for her family, but rather in terms of the affection and care she received:

> My mother let me have my way at most everything, [but] I've never been a problem child. I was never a spoiled child. I never give my mother and father no kind of trouble. . . . My mother always said I was real kind.

When she was twenty, she married Edward, who also brought to the union an illegitimate child, Herbert, the same age as Dorothy. Eleven children have been born to this couple over the twenty-two years of their marriage. Della Mae never gave her babies to her daughters, and she even assumed the major responsibility for caring for the four illegitimate children born to her oldest daughter Madeline (twenty-two) before Madeline moved out of the apartment at the Housing Authority's request. Madeline, who went to live with a maternal aunt for three or four years, is the only child Della Mae ever "farmed out," even though she was "her father's favorite."

Finally, Betty Re Buchanan (forty-nine) expresses her great joy over not having had the responsibility of caring for children pushed off on her while she was coming up. She was raised by her older sisters and they spoiled her. When she married, she brought one illegitimate child, Tilly, with her, and her husband went out of his way to care for their children. This is the only instance where there is evidence of a husband paying such attention to the children. Tilly was born when Betty Re was fourteen. Betty Re married when she was thirty-one and over the eighteen years of their marriage she has given birth to a total of twelve children:

> I didn't have too much responsibility . . . because my sisters pampered me a lot. . . . My mother died when I was about three. I lived with my sisters till Tilly was about two [Betty Re herself was sixteen]. . . . I didn't ever have to take care of Tilly. I *never* had to take care of no kids. [The neighbors would ask my sister] "Why don't you make Betty Re take care of those kids?" and she would say "Betty Re don't have no kids."

The responsibility for caring for babies has come to Betty Re more since she has been a grandmother, but even now she has not taken over two of the three grandchildren, who are cared for mainly by their mothers. One grandson, Ellwood (two), however, has become her favorite. One has the impression that he receives more attention than any of her own children ever received from her. Her conception of mothering tends toward indulgency. She "cares" in being able to provide her children with whatever they ask for (more an ideal than a reality) and in treating her children affectionately.

Generally speaking, not only did the first born spend more of their early lives caring for children, but they now express greater ambivalence toward their own children and are more inclined to "give their babies" to an older daughter, thus perpetuating the cycle another generation. The middle and last born show a greater inclination to "adopt" their grandchildren, and thus experience motherhood when they have in fact become grandmothers. The last born mothers show greater tendencies to indulge their children.

Hertha Reise suggests that the grandmother's "greed for babies" is a factor pressing her to encourage her daughter's sexual licentiousness. She argues:

> Due to the lack of opportunity for maturation the earlier born children of a girl or at times a couple are just by-products of "sex play." The children's neglect reflects the mother's lack of readiness for motherhood—its responsibilities and enjoyments. While the teenage mother is avid for sexual gratification, the thirty to thirty-five year old grandmother is an insatiable consumer of grandchildren regardless of what it does to the child. . . . For the experience of womanhood the disarmed young mother will rely on mere sexuality at the expense of a more complete experience which includes motherhood. . . . In a decade and a half the daughter will have to catch up with the experience

> of motherhood and regain a more complete experience of womanhood, as well as the idea of self, at the expense of her daughter.[2]

Reise does not consider the matter of birth order. The data on these ten mothers, however, suggest that this grim and vicious cycle is more characteristic of later-born women. The first-born legitimate ones have been too overexposed to child care to seek further gratification in their grandchildren. Table II summarizes this experience in caring for children.

Table II CHILD BEARING EXPERIENCE

Name	Present Age	Age at Birth of First Child	Age at Birth of Second Child	Age at Marriage	Age at Birth of First Daughter	Age at Birth of First Legitimate Daughter	Age at Birth of Last Child	Age at Birth of First Grandchild	No. years/No Children
First Born:									
Lotta W.	47	19	20	18	27	27	34	45	1.56
Dorothy B.	40	17	24	25	17	23	34	38	2.13
Tilly H.	33	15	16	14	26	26	30	—	1.50
Alberta B.	31	22	25	25	22	25	27	—	1.66
Middle Child:									
Leona W.	50	18	23	17	18	18	34	35	2.29
Mae Apple F.	40	19	25	20	19	24	39	—	2.00
Ethyl P.	34	15	16	15	15	18	25	32	2.00
Lilly P.	33	22	23	20	22	22	27	—	1.00
Last Born:									
Betty Re B.	55	14	32	32	14	32	43	47	1.50
Della Mae P.	42	15	19	20	15	23	42	33	2.00

OBSERVATIONS ON THE CARE OF INFANTS

While it is probable that more children will be born in four of the ten households, there are, at present, only four infants in the house-

[2] Hertha Reise, *Heal the Hurt Child* (Chicago: The University of Chicago Press, 1962), pp. 60–61.

holds. Three of these are grandchildren living in the three-generation household of the Buchanans. While six of the mothers are also grandmothers, only in the cases of the Buchanans and Pattersons do the grandchildren spend a considerable portion of their time with their grandparents. Danella Patterson (one) does not spend as much time with the Pattersons as she does with the Buchanans, her maternal grandparents. The Buchanans also have two other grandchildren, Ellwood and Sue, by their son Junior, who stay with them from time to time.

Although Betty Re managed to put most of the baby-sitting off on her children, she nevertheless has her own conception of how babies should be cared for:

> Well at least don't get them in the habit of holding them. Kind of space it out because most of them get used to your lap and your arms. They know when they're in your arms. . . . Most people say, "Oh, let them holler, he'll go to sleep." But I just don't like that. Usually when he's good and full, clean and dry then most likely he'll lay there and play or go on back to sleep. When they wake up if you feed them and clean them up they'll go on back to sleep. I don't believe in letting them cry. . . . A lot of mothers let them holler till they're red in the face and can't hardly get their breath. . . . The kids wake up early in the morning, around six or six-thirty. I always made it a rule to get up and feed it, dry it and take the things off his bed and air his bed out and after we feed them and play with them. . . . We put our kids on baby cereal as soon as they come home from the hospital. . . . When you're feeding them out of a spoon when they're small like that they won't take it very well. If you fix it in the bottle . . . they take it much better. [For a formula] we used Pet milk and Karo syrup and sterilized water. Then we play with them a while and then we give them a bath about ten or eleven and then give them their bottle of milk and put them to bed. . . . Then they go back to sleep and sleep to maybe about twelve-thirty or one and then they wake up. We play with them again and give them their lunch like those strained vegetables, we give them the formula with that. They usually don't eat much out of a spoon. . . . A baby five weeks old could probably eat five or six times out of one jar . . . of baby food. . . . A lot of people start

> the kids at the table, but I don't start the kids from the table because *I still* give Ellwood baby food. I feed them something like mashed potatoes . . . mashed bananas . . . eggs. . . . Maybe we'd get up and dry them once a night because when they're wet they're awful uncomfortable and I feel like you can dry them without waking them up. . . . And while I dry them I put the bottle in their mouth. When I get ready to go out I take the bottle out of their mouth because the baby might strangle. I don't like for people to put a bottle in the baby's mouth and go away. . . . So I think if you keep them fed and dry they'll be good babies.

Ellwood never received such attention, but then he was not her child. He remained the center of attention of the Buchanan household until the arrival of Sue and Danella. Understandably, the quick change in interest upset him and he was on several occasions seen to strike out at the babies in anger. The Buchanans say he's jealous. Now he wanders around the house, sucking on whatever object he is carrying and trying to once again get "in" on things.

During the summer of 1965, Mary, Ellwood's mother, moved into the Buchanan apartment in order to make Gerald Buchanan fully aware of his parental responsibilities. Della and Dora, Gerald's sisters, say, however, that they like Ellwood and Mary and wanted to have them around, and Mary admits that she gets a great deal of help in caring for Ellwood. She stayed until Thanksgiving 1965. While there she and Ellwood had a room to themselves. Gerald slept with his brothers most of the time.

As the first child born in several years in the Buchanan family, Ellwood receives a great amount of attention from most everyone but his mother. Quite often he was placed in the sole care of the Buchanan children or Betty Re. Considerably less frequently, Mary's mother took care of him—to some extent because Ethyl worked part-time during the latter half of 1965, and also because of a subdued but real animosity between Betty Re and Ethyl, stemming from Betty Re's opinion that Ethyl's constant contact with boyfriends was a bad influence on Mary. Betty Re remarked that Mary had asked to come to live with them because she did not like her mother's boyfriend. During the first year of his life, Ellwood was held by almost everyone in the household so much so that he was rarely seen crawling. He went from "in arm" to walking with very little time on all fours. He is showered with affection constantly and rarely disciplined. Even when he spills things all over the living room, Betty Re makes light of it. Mary maintains that only Della and Gerald can discipline him now and make him mind.

Ellwood was fed from the table quite early, and sometimes the menu was not appropriate for a toothless baby. The scene is in Mary's dining room on the occasion of a late lunch or early dinner in March; the time is about three o'clock:

> Annie Lou held Ellwood on her lap now facing out and Ellwood grabbed for plates on the table and banged around. He played with keys and generally squeaked and squealed. He sucked on his pacifier. Once he tried to get up on the table, but Annie Lou prevented this. . . . Mary did not make one friendly overture to Ellwood during this entire time in her apartment. She was quite indifferent to him and I had the impression that he was looking at her every now and then as if trying to recognize who she was. Shortly after we were there Annie Lou gave Ellwood to Louise, Mary's younger sister, and she carried him on the side of her hip to the kitchen where she found a cold dish [custard size] of spaghetti. . . . She took the food in a regular size teaspoon and shoveled it into his mouth. . . . He attempted to chew or suck on it and passed it finally down his throat.

From time to time a bit of resentment flares up between the female members of the Buchanan household over Mary's shirking of her responsibility for Ellwood's care. When asked how often he was bathed, Annie responded, "He's not bathed unless I bathe him," and Mary, after some further joking remarks, admitted that he was bathed "maybe" once a month. After Annie Lou left, Mary retorted that the only reason Annie Lou was holding the baby now was in order to get out of work.

Ellwood's father likes to tease him. This teasing is sometimes a means of "getting to" Mary, as on this occasion:

> Mary was rocking him back and forth on the table and Gerald, in order to get into the game, decided to push Ellwood and Mary's heads together resulting in a mild hurt to both. Mary was quite angry and Ellwood began to whine a little, but Gerald was quite delighted. He would pull Ellwood's arm saying, "I'm going

> to break this." And then growl. Ellwood would respond with a little short cry. His father delighted in getting this little cry out of him. . . . Ellwood apparently was not at all sure whether his father was serious in this or not. The little cry I took to be a cry of alarm. Gerald continued teasing in this way for several minutes and Mary would take the side of Ellwood when Gerald would stop growling. She would whisper in Ellwood's ear that he should hit his father, "Hit him, Ellwood. Hit him, Ellwood."

Gerald sees such behavior as a way of helping his son become a man, just as he feels that it is perfectly all right for Ellwood to drink a bit of beer from his glass. This is a characteristic mode of interaction between father and son, and leads one to surmise that Gerald's control over Ellwood stems from the latter's fear of him.

Stewart Frazier was breast fed by his mother, Mae Apple, until he was well over a year old. Being the least urbanized of all the families, the Fraziers have not yet given up this rural tradition. Mae Apple feels no embarrassment about feeding him in the presence of strangers. She holds him tenderly against her breast and talks cooingly to him while her older children gather around.

When he is not being fed, he is handled by all the members of the family as they pass him from arm to arm, or he is left to play on a pallet on the floor while one or more of the older children watch. While she was breast feeding Stewart, Mae Apple did not let her older daughters, Rosie Joe (thirteen) and Mary Re (twelve), do much more than baby-sit for him. However, after she weaned him by putting iodine on her nipples, she "gave him" to Rosie Joe. Now Rosie Joe changes his diapers, bathes him, feeds him, and in general looks after his welfare. She does this with a great deal of tenderness and with considerable assistance from her younger sisters. Only Lester, her father (thirty-seven), and her older brother Richard (fifteen) seem to have little to do with Stewart. They are not hostile toward the baby; they are just not as interested in holding, feeding, talking to, and playing with the youngest member of the family. The Fraziers have three boys under the age of five, but neither Samuel (four) nor John (two) seems to be jealous of this younger brother who has deprived them of the center of attention. The interaction between the younger children is generally affectionate:

Her baby was on a pallet in the living room and the next oldest child, John, was taking care of Stewart. There is a great deal of pleasure and fun expressed between these two. Samuel was providing Stewart with toys and it seemed as though he was getting a big kick out of play with his baby brother.

PRE-SCHOOL PROBLEMS

Both Richard Parvin and Louise Billit were two years old when the study of their families began. Both exhibited abnormal behavior and were slow to pick up speech. Louise, at the age of four, still does not speak. She whines and whimpers but makes no effort to speak. Richard, now five, has the beginnings of speech but is still a very withdrawn child. These two children are only two examples of a much larger problem faced by almost every family in the project—that of having to rear children with severe handicaps.[3]

Richard is ordinarily found to be very dirty, quite often with a cold, and normally either lying motionless on the sofa in the living room or else standing staring wide-eyed at the activities of his older siblings. Lilly Parvin states that he has always been sick—"he keeps a cold." His poor health is made more difficult to bear by the dirt he accumulates because of his mother's neglect. Often he will spend the day in dirty diapers, fouling everything he sits upon, and no one will change him. Lilly wonders about Rich:

> I don't know. I don't believe Rich is happy all the time . . . his face is too serious all the time. He won't stay clean.

In her confused state of mind, his condition is not her responsibility:

[3] In these ten families, for example, seven children have handicaps requiring special treatment from doctors: Rachael Perry (thirteen) has severe hearing loss; Willie Mae Parvin (nine) was expelled from school and ordered to take a psychiatric examination because she would not talk to peers or to her teacher; Richard (five) is slow developing speech and is very withdrawn; Clinton Buchanan (eight) is an extremely aggressive child and has a low IQ (fifties); his sister Annette (eight) has an IQ of fifty-six; Louise Billit has been under doctor's care since she had pneumonia at the age of one, and does not speak at the age of four; Carl Handy has extremely weak eye muscles requiring strong corrective glasses at the age of three. These are only the most obvious symptoms, and do not include the general ill health of the children during the winter months.

> I think my dad had something to do with that, 'cause one time I was up there and I was looking at Rich and I told him, I say, "Rich is getting to be a bad little boy," and seems he tried to train Rich [at using the toilet].

Her sisters are also accused of having made Rich the way he is—the unhappy child that will not stay clean. Lilly further emphasizes her detachment from Rich by holding him as one would hold a sack of potatoes, expressing little tenderness in her touch. She was pregnant with Rich when she and her husband separated for the last time. Since that abrupt separation her illness has been worse, according to the account given by her father.

Lilly is quite concerned with Rich because he is not toilet trained at two. She gets angry when he won't go to the toilet. She claims that he is the worst problem she has had in this matter:

> I don't never have no trouble with my babies, because most of the time now I take my babies and I train them when they are little babies.

She talks about a routine that is observable in her household only infrequently:

> I fix their breakfast about eight in the morning, then I give them a bath and make sure they ain't buggy or nothing and sometimes I make a little pallet and put it on the floor for them. . . . And if they get buggy, I put them outdoors under a tree. Then I come on out there and sit around for a while. . . . Sometimes I take them for a walk, too. Then I clean them up at night time, then I put them to bed early and I sit up and watch television.

This conversation reflects what she does for her children when she is reasonably well. When she is not, there is much less care. She normally does not fix more than one meal a day, usually at breakfast time. The children fix whatever they want during the rest of the day. On those occasions when the one meal she prepares comes later in the day, it will be something more substantial than a breakfast. (The common pattern in the project is for a mother to fix the main meal of the day in the evening.) She does not clean the children during the day, and, as a result, all but the oldest are extremely dirty. Even so, much of the responsibility for the care of Richard is placed upon the girls. Even the youngest, Barbara (six), was observed giving Rich a bath. The oldest girl, Kim (nine), is the major source of discipline. She and her younger sister Stephanie are responsible for the procurement and distribution of whatever food the children have during the day.

Louise Billit presents a problem quite different from Rich's. The following observation was made of Louise at the age of three:

> Mr. Billit proceeded to put Louise's shoes on. He treated her very tenderly. He put her socks on and then her shoes. She was wearing some red overshoes in the house previously. When Louise had her shoes put on she walked around the apartment and bounced back and forth on the club chair like I have observed the Parvin children doing. Her walk, I noticed, was a rather stiff, mechanical kind of walk. She holds her back exceptionally straight and walks almost as a mechanical doll would walk, a kind of toy soldier march.

Louise is the Billit's only legitimate child. Mr. Billit gives in to her screaming demands and does not make any attempt to discipline her when she gets into things around the house. His wife Alliena, however, gets very angry at Louise and is constantly shouting at her to keep out of things. Rarely does she correct the child's behavior, however. Louise is constantly on the move:

> A characteristic of Louise's activity is the clapping of hands. She seems to enjoy this and it is one of the few things that she does that can be called playing. Most of the other activities could be interpreted as exploration or meddling. However, she does clap her hands and bounce her back off the club chairs and sometimes does both at the same time. This seems to please her, but most of the time she has a rather vacant stare on her face and a kind of strange look of longing as she goes from adult to adult seeking comfort of some kind. Once she wanted to crawl on my legs but Mrs. Billit picked her up and gave her a "horsie" ride on her leg.

She appears to be very much at the center of the conflict that constantly rages between her parents, and is the victim of her mother's expressed dislike of children—which resulted, as we have seen, from too much exposure to children too early in life as the first-born child. In the Billit household, also, much of the care of the baby falls to the oldest girl, Camella (nine).

A notable characteristic of the younger children in the project is their ease in showing affection and their almost inexhaustible desire to receive it. Most of the youngsters will come up and sit on a stranger's lap, hug him, and generally court his attention—if he shows the slightest interest in them. They provide a welcome contrast to the apparent hostility of the older children. Whatever affection is shown by others is warmly received. This is more understandable when it is remembered that these are the members of the family who are making the difficult adjustment involved in giving up the "baby" role. In comparison with their younger siblings, who are at the center of the family's interests, these youngsters are starved for affection.

While most mothers and older children express great warmth and affection toward the younger members of the family, there is, as has been noted, a basis for an extreme amount of hostility. This hostility remains latent in most situations, but is openly exposed in others—as in the case of the mentally ill Mrs. Parvin. It also erupts in those instances when parents become angry and fear that they will lose control of themselves, as in the cases of Alliena Billit and Dorothy Brown. The hostility may stem from the excessive demands made upon them as first-born children who had to care for their mother's children; it may result from having a child while still in one's middle teens and not being able to escape caring for that child; or it may derive from the anxiety incipient in the unpredictable marital situations, where one is likely to be left with the children at any time. Thus, while children are undoubtedly a mark of maturity and status for the young girl, and while they are evidence of the superiority of the female sex, and are therefore *overtly* loved to the point of overindulgence, this strong *covert* current of hostility is very much a part of the orientation toward children in the project. Youngsters must cope with this as well as with the burdens of ill health and the social and racial handicaps of poverty and discrimination. They must do this often in the context of an unstable home life, where one may be sent off to live with a relative for a number of years, where one has relatives living at home for a number of years (providing not only playmates, but also rivals for parental affection and the other necessary and scarce items of existence), and where it is not unlikely that mother or father will desert. In the context of such stress, it seems remarkable that the young child coming up has any chance at all of developing an adequate, if not wholly healthy, personality. The very "looseness" of the internal family structure forces one to adapt to the fact that people are unpredictable. This has some positive value in this context, however, for it trains one for the encounter with the world of the street.

THE GRADE SCHOOL YEARS

In comparison to their younger siblings, the grade schoolers in the project are the objects of considerably less attention and affection. They are out of the house for a large portion of the day. Parents here as elsewhere are generally glad to get them out of the house. Forty-three children fall into this age group.

The younger of these children—say those between six and ten years old—are the source of few problems for their parents in contrast to the older children. They do not require as much care as they did formerly. They attract comparatively little parental attention as they go about the business of growing up, largely under the influence of their peers and siblings. As they enter their teens, however, they emerge once again as objects of concern for their parents. This concern now focuses around the consequences of sexual behavior resulting in pregnancy, deviant behavior resulting in police records, and the heightened concern of the parents that they begin to give evidence of being able to "go for themselves"—a concern that is aroused because by this time it has become obvious to most parents that their children are behind in the school system, and are continually tempted to drop out. Despite these awakening awarenesses, the grade school years are perhaps the most trouble free of any periods of these youngsters' lives and represent the years in which they are, for the most part, freed of responsibilities in the home and allowed to grow up in relative anonymity.

Of the forty-three children who fall into this group, thirty-five are middle children, four are last-born children, two are first-born, and two are first-born legitimate girls. The problems of the first-born girls here also focus around the responsibility they are given in the home of caring for their younger siblings and in doing the work of the household. In some instances, the role of being the baby as last born has been considerably modified by this age, due to the arrival of grandchildren in the household and their consequent capture of the center of attention.

Kim Parvin is nine. Her problems as the first born are heightened by the severe handicap imposed on the family by her mother's mental illness. Nevertheless, at eight she is observed to be a guiding force in this family world. One morning Lilly, her mother, got up first and called to her oldest daughter, Kim:

> Kim get up now. You got to help me this morning. You got to help me; I'm late. [Kim continues for a few moments to lie in bed, then she gets up and trudges off to the bathroom] . . . Kim, you give Rich a bath now, do you hear?
>
> *Kim* [from the bathroom]: All right!

Lilly calls upon Kim a great deal. At nine Kim cooks nearly as much as her mother, does more of the shopping, is frequently called upon to discipline her siblings and care for her baby brother. According to the children, she is the only one in the household who can stand up to Lilly's unwanted boyfriend, Ronnie. To an amazing extent Kim runs the house. Her mother is very ambivalent about this. She complains, "Kim wants to be the boss of this house," but she constantly makes use of her services. Lilly has recurring dreams about Kim. In one she and Kim are chased by lions, or sometimes bears. They are on a mountain and trying to get away from the animals. They run across a flimsy bridge over a stream and then Lilly wakes up. In another she is anxious about Kim's falling into a lake. From across the lake she shouts a warning and then wakes up. In both it seems there is a repressed desire to see that Kim is dead, perhaps because of the threat she poses to Lilly's weakened self-esteem. Other mothers more healthy than Lilly admit to no such ambivalence, but rather view it as fitting and proper that the oldest assume the responsibility.

This is particularly true of Alliena Billit, herself a first-born child, and her daughter Camella (nine). When she is home from school, Camella can cook most meats, make bread "from scratch," and assume the major chore of caring for her younger half-sister Louise. She generally presents herself as a very responsible person. Once, when she was being taken to a bus that would take her to camp, she was given a dollar for spending money as a gift. Two months later, she came one evening with a dollar and said that she wanted to pay it back. When told that the money had not been intended as a loan, she insisted that she would rather pay it back now so she could borrow again when she really needed it. This behavior is in marked contrast to that of her father, who has borrowed several dollars "as a loan" and has yet to pay them back. Camella is not his child and she is not the object of his affection. As an illegitimate first child, she has never known her biological father and receives a great deal of anger from her "stepfather."

The situation in the case of Rosie Joe Frazier (thirteen) is much the same as that described above, even though she has an older brother, Richard, who does not help out much around the house, but who does provide the family with a very great service in that he is the most literate member of the family. Rosie Joe is now the person mainly responsible for the care of her youngest brother, Stewart (one).

In the case of Tilly Handy, five boys were born to her, three of whom are only half-brothers, and her family lives with her grandparents, where there are several older girls to care for the younger members of both households. As the oldest daughter, however, she does receive some preferential treatment from her mother, and is greatly admired by her younger sisters and brothers.

The middle-born children seem to have more diversified problems and pleasures. Stephanie Parvin at the age of eight has already become a "fast" girl, in her mother's eyes, who plays tantalizing games with boys, and whose ready wit gets her out of trouble. Yet of all the Parvin children, Stephanie seems the healthiest. She likes "to play rope and penny ball and ride bikes . . . go swimming, *be clean,* write . . . play on the merry-go-round and be on the sliding board, ride roller coasters . . . and horsies round and round." She likes "watermelon, going to the show, playing cowboys and playing around." Of course, she does not do many of these things often because her family is so poor and her mother overly suspicious of her activities. As the second oldest daughter in the family, she does not have quite the status of her older sister Kim, but manages to put all of her brothers properly in their places. She sleeps with the oldest of these brothers, Jerry (six). When playing with him in the living room she mimics the sex act. This greatly annoys her mother, who takes it as long as she can, and then attempts to strike her, but usually Stephanie manages to run away.

Her identification as a female is not as oriented toward child care as her sister's, and the reputation for being "fast" is reinforced by her constant concern with sexual themes in songs and play. This little girl, her mother contends, will be some "hot mama" when she grows up. In the context of her home she is learning adaptive behavior for the street. She was once asked, "What is a nice girl?" She answered with the help of her siblings:

Nice girls be clean and mind your mama.

Q: Do nice girls get married?

No.

Q: Don't you want to get married?

No.

Q: How come?

My mama say if you don't have a husband you don't get any children.

Q: Do you have a boyfriend?

I don't got no boyfriend, but Jerry got a girlfriend . . . named Pig. . . . We saw Jerry try to kiss her.

Willie Mae: And Stephanie tried to kiss Leonard.

Stephanie: Jerry . . . went up to Pig and stick his thing in her.

Jerry: I didn't do dat for real.

Stephanie: Oh yes he did, oh he did. We were there.

Leonard [using a pole to indicate his penis]: He do dis, he do dis, he done it to this new girl, we saw him. [Imitates the act of sexual intercourse with the huge pole using Willie Mae who is sitting on the bed as his target] And Stephanie come on top of these fellas.

[At this point Stephanie gets mad at Leonard. She runs over to him and pulls his pants halfway down, grabs hold of his penis, and punches his testicles, at the same time trying to take his pants all the way off. Leonard bursts into a screaming cry and runs behind the bedpost, where he remains sucking two fingers for the better part of fifteen minutes, refusing to speak.]

Q: What's the matter with Leonard?

Stephanie: He just gets mad cause I told about him and that girl.

At this age Stephanie really doesn't know if she is a nice girl or not. Her mother keeps labeling her as a bad girl, and she behaves appropriately, but she has not yet fully accepted the label. Once, knowing her mother's professed admiration for the Sanctified church and its strict discipline, Stephanie asked, "Are you sanctified?" When told "no," she giggled and replied, "I ain't either."

This playing at sex, which is more obvious in the Parvin household than in others in the project, is nonetheless a common, overt theme. Sex is regarded as natural, and as long as it is done with some discretion (that is, not in plain view of adults) little is done to guide its progression. If Stephanie follows the pattern, by the time she is thirteen she will have had sexual relations with a boy and, in the assessment of most persons in the project, will be pregnant by fourteen.[4]

Sexuality is not discussed in the homes. Most boys and girls discover it for themselves, and discuss their discoveries with their close friends, the girls quite frequently with older sisters. As a result, there is little understanding about sexual matters despite great practical experience. At least two of the girls who have borne children assert that they never knew where children came from before they had their first child.

Annie Lou is the fourth legitimate daughter born to the Buchanans. At thirteen she is quite a terror in her own right. She does care for her younger siblings on occasion, particularly her nephew Ellwood (having been made an "auntie" at the ripe old age of twelve). But this is not a burdensome matter to her. Her concerns are more in avoiding household responsibilities and enjoying her peer relationships, particularly the growing discovery of herself as an attractive young girl and the differences that that makes to boys. Annie Lou is far behind in school, and this makes her quite conspicuous as she sits in her sixth

[4] Jerome Stromberg, "Perspectives on Pathology, Socialization, Religion, and World View of (Project) Residents" (St. Louis: Internal Working Paper Number Five, The Social Science Institute of Washington University, 1966), p. 23.

grade class and towers above her classmates. She does not have a good record of attendance and is most frequently at home "sick" watching TV. She and her sister Geraldine (fourteen) have been "farmed out" to live with a friend of the family in the suburbs for the major part of their younger lives. Geraldine did not know that Mrs. Buchanan was in fact her mother until she was five. Even after she found out she continued to stay with her "foster" parents until she was about ten. Geraldine lived with twelve other foster children in this home. She felt loved however:

> I was the only girl. . . . I was going to be adopted but I wasn't.
>
> *Q:* What happened?
>
> Well, mother dear, I guess she took the money back because she didn't want me to be adopted. Mama had paid $50.00. That's what I heard. She had paid $50.00 and signed some papers and I didn't get adopted. I just stayed there until I got a certain age.

Now Geraldine prefers to live with her foster parents because she is permitted to do what she wants out there and has to help out with the housework when she lives with the Buchanans. She spends the weekends and the summers in the suburbs even now:

> I've got eleven brothers and I've got feelings for them. I got one more sister, Connie. She lives in the suburbs too with her little son and daughter. I call them my niece [and nephew] because they're just like my niece, and I feel the same way for them that I feel for Danella [her sister's child]. It ain't no difference in them to me.

Middle children seem to be "farmed out" more than their legitimate older or younger sisters, a characteristic they share with their illegitimate half-brothers and sisters who (particularly if they are first born) go to live elsewhere. They too express preference for the foster home over their own, stating that life is much easier there. But they also express, as does Geraldine, some resentment of their parents for having shipped them off. Geraldine calls her "foster" parents "mama" and "papa," although she differentiates between her foster mother and her mother by calling the latter *mother dear.* Geraldine is very much a "loner" in the Buchanan household, in large measure because of her not having lived with her brothers and sisters very much. She keeps to herself and concentrates on her studying, a trait not typical of the Buchanans.

THE HIGH SCHOOL YEARS

The most common dilemma faced by the high school girl is poised by the conflict over "career" versus motherhood. In the ghetto, however, this has much more of an ominous overtone than in the world of the middle class. The problem is accentuated by the fact that many girls have had sexual relations by the time they enter high school. It is considered the normal thing to do to "please" your boyfriend. They are, however, largely ignorant of effective contraceptive techniques, fearful of using them, or conduct their sexual activities in situations where several contraceptive devices would be useless because they require that lovemaking be planned in advance. In the case of seven out of ten of the mothers and five of the fifteen teenage daughters in these families, children out of wedlock resulted from this "natural" lovemaking.

An Extreme Case of a Common Choice

The problems faced in handling sexuality and the boyfriend are dramatically portrayed in the following account given by Madeline Patterson who, at the age of twenty-three, has given birth to five illegitimate children, four of whom are still alive. She had her first child, Bootsie, when she was fourteen while still going to school:

> Bootsie's father Donnie [nineteen] wasn't going to school when I met him. Him and some other fellows used to be down by the school when school let out. Every afternoon he would chase me home and then he started coming over to the school during recess when we would be outside taking exercises. One night Louis R. gave a dance. He lived two flights over us on the sixth floor. Donnie was there. L. R. introduced me to Donnie. Donnie would come down to see me. Sometimes I would be downstairs with one of my sisters and he would come and sit on the bench with me. We'd talk and everything. After that we started going

> together. He gave me his ring. *I didn't know anything about sex or where babies came from because didn't nobody tell me.* We had been going together for about nine months. This lady I used to baby-sit for she didn't mind me having company or nothing like that as long as they leave at a reasonable time if she wasn't home. Donnie'd come down there and sometimes my sister or my brother would come down. This particular night he asked me and I refused and one thing led to another. He wanted to know "Why?" *I told him I was scared.* He said it wasn't going to hurt. I told him I didn't know and I didn't want to find out. We got to wrestling and—this is sort of embarrassing—he just kept on pestering me. He told me I didn't care anything for him and things like that. He said he wouldn't let anything happen to me or something similar to that. This went on for about an hour and a half. I said "Okay" and that was that.

Madeline was in the eighth grade at the time and the school nurse finally had to send her home. "I just kept getting bigger and I had to leave my skirt unfastened and I slept a lot." The principal called her mother, her mother called Donnie's mother. The juvenile officer came to talk to Madeline. "He explained that I could have Donnie locked up for statutory rape. But he said if I had pressed charges against him that I had to go to jail too or something for overnight. I told him no." At the time they were planning on getting married—that is, they talked about it in an offhand manner:

> At the time Donnie was running around with a rowdy crowd and they was forever into fights and things . . . and he stayed in jail more than he did out at that time. So I just told mother that I didn't want to marry him.

Her mother consented to her wishes, but her father felt she ought to marry. After she became pregnant, she saw Donnie only on the street:

> Before I had my baby I couldn't stand Donnie. I guess because he was the cause of my being pregnant. I could see him walking down the street and I'd get angry and want to cry.

Her parents discussed the matter of her pregnancy out of her hearing and concluded that they would look into the matter of sending her to a special home where she could give birth to the child. This was apparently her father's alternative to marrying. "I believe he was more hurt and disappointed than she was." However, after a visit to the home convinced her mother that she could not send her daughter to such a place, it was decided that Madeline should not go. Her mother mostly took care of her first child.

Madeline began going out with boys again shortly after she gave birth: "It wasn't as if the baby was holding me down or anything because if I wanted to go any place my mother she would usually watch the baby for me." The kids at the dances she went to, however, "looked like my little sisters and brothers." She preferred Dave (nineteen) who didn't like to go out. Dave gave her her second child, Carol, when she was fifteen. She does not know how she became pregnant:

> I don't remember. To tell the truth I actually don't remember. I think maybe the reason I can't remember is because when I found out I was pregnant, I was so hurt and disappointed and everything else and I didn't know just what to do. I thought about giving the baby away when I had it. But my mother talked me out of that. And I just tried to forget everything about Carol's father and Carol and how it happened, because Dave and I we was going to get married, but I found out that he was already married and I didn't know this. He hadn't never gotten a divorce from his first wife. . . . His aunt told me [this].

She did not think about abortions:

> One of the girls I used to go to school with was telling me something that I could take or something, but I was scared. . . . I thought of other things such as leaving home and things like that and leaving my first child with Donnie's mother since she wanted her from the beginning.

Her mother again interceded for the child: "She said that she raised us and she never had gave a child of hers away." Since Madeline was herself born before wedlock when her mother was nineteen, this argument had some weight.

Madeline's second child, Carol, came after only seven months of pregnancy, and Madeline became very sick after the delivery. Her mother took care of this child also. "I was afraid I would drop her or something." She never saw Dave again until Carol was ten months old. After Carol was born Madeline left home and has been living on her own with her children for about seven years now.

When she was sixteen she met Jay (twenty-three). Jay was the first boyfriend to regularly support her, giving her about fifteen or twenty dollars every week, usually on Friday or Saturday. Jay left suspecting, unjustifiably, that she was pregnant:

> He asked me if I was pregnant and I told him "No." Then he told me a friend of mine told him I was going to the doctor to get rid of his baby. I told him that was a lie, because I wasn't pregnant, and if I was I wouldn't do anything like that. I would rather have it and give it away than do anything like that.
>
> *Q:* Were you in love with Jay?
>
> I think so. The reason I say that is after that I just didn't trust men. I mean I don't really trust them now, but it seems like he destroyed something in me. I don't know.

About a year afterward she met her next boyfriend, Raymond, the father of Val, born when Madeline was nearly eighteen. Until she met Raymond she stayed around the house moping. Raymond is a friend of the family and a constant drinker, even though he suffers from bleeding ulcers. "We all have to go sometime." He is divorced and in his late twenties. Raymond still visits with Madeline's parents and drinks quite often with her father. He had proposed marriage seriously, gotten her to the license bureau, but she backed out:

> . . . I think it was more or less the idea of getting married. I was thinking about the *types of marriages they had on television and in the books.*[5] I know it's not like that. I always said I would never get married because lots of men do their wives so bad. I wanted to, but when the time come, I just didn't want to.

At about this time in her life her father left her mother for the second or third time since the family had moved to the city, and her

[5] Characteristically, women in the project watch television a good part of the day and prefer "soap operas" and programs with plots related to domestic intrigues. Many will say they like these because it lets them think about someone else's problems for a change or because the shows are so much like real life that they can readily identify with the characters.

mother was stuck with a very sick daughter and no food in the house. Madeline, once the favorite of her father, now despises him for what he has done to her mother.

Since Carol, Madeline has had three more children. John was born when she was twenty and Willie shortly thereafter. Willie died in infancy. Mark's father left before Madeline knew she was pregnant. Willie's father—like Carol's—was already married. She remembers that Willie's father, Cal, used to get confused and call her by his wife's name, Sally:

> Some nights he would be asleep and he would get to talking in his sleep. He said, "Sally, Madeline has a little girl named Carol also and she's just as big as our girl." . . . He said, "Sally, I don't want to hurt Madeline. . . . Sally, I'm not going to see you any more because Madeline is nice and I don't want to hurt her because she's good to me."

Cal was twenty-six when he first met Madeline. He talked of marriage, as is the appropriate thing to do when "making out," but Madeine thought she was in love with him. "Val and Willie were the only two babies I really wanted," but Cal got sent up to the federal penitentiary for three years, and that more or less ended the affair.

At the present time Madeline is going with Stan, twenty-four. He is single but has two children by a girl he had been going with. He has been going with Madeline for about three years. He gets paid every two weeks and gives her twenty-five to thirty dollars, maybe more. Most of their enjoyment is in the context of her home where his concern extends to the children as well. She muses: "They seem warmer towards him than they do perhaps to their own father." Marriage is something that she is still looking for, but she is not certain if Stan is the man to marry:

> Marriage don't necessarily have to be perfect. The only thing I'm looking for and the only thing I ask is that they respect my kids and me and do whatever they can for us.

An Alternative Pattern

With examples such as Madeline's always before them, and the awareness that men are not dependable, a minority—but an interesting minority—of girls attempt to put off engaging in sexual intercourse with boys until they are out of high school. Madeline's younger sister Glennora, eighteen, has this to say:

I had my first boyfriend when I started in high school. That was in 1964. He was really a boyfriend. The others weren't really boyfriends.

Q: Well, when you really become boyfriend and girlfriend what does that mean?

I don't know. Things change so much in years. It seems like sometimes if a boy asks you to be his woman, well, you say "Yeah," and you all go together. I guess because you all like each other. Then again some boys, like if they be talking to you . . . just keep talking to you, well you all just take it for granted that you all go together instead of him asking you and he'll treat you like you're his girlfriend or somebody he likes. But then again some people just go with people for to be doing something. You know, they might not really like them and they just go with them. Like the pimps. The boy pimps be calling their girlfriends and they don't really like them . . . they just be going with them to get some money. So people take it in different ways.

Q: Well, how do you take it?

When I call somebody my boyfriend, it would be somebody that I like. I might not like them a great deal, but I do care for them. . . .

Q: Have you done it with a boy?

No I haven't . . . because I really haven't liked anybody enough to really go through those changes and when I do I want it to be with someone I really like and who really likes me. And furthermore that's my pride. *When I give that away I haven't got anything else to offer a boy.* . . . I'm not ready for that type of thing. . . .

Q: What about Harris [her boyfriend]? Does he understand?

Yes he do. Because he understands that I'm trying to get out of school and I guess he knows I want the better things in life and I guess he wants to see that I try to get it. . . . We have been going together for two years and nothing has happened.

For Glennora the notion of being in love—really in love—is mixed with a concern to get through school and establish her own earning power. She is well aware of the fact that "love is an everyday word" in her neighborhood, and she sees "how boys are doing these girls today . . . getting them pregnant and going on to somebody else." This awareness is reinforced by her sister's experience and her own concern about marriage stemming from the very disappointing experience of her parents' marriage.

Dora Buchanan (fifteen) has also the example of her old sister Della to consider, but her concern about not having relations with a boy is more a matter of propriety:

> I don't think it's right, not yet anyway, because it's too many boys these days going with girls and you know they'll go out and talk about everything they do with this girl. And it's really not no right place to do it. I mean some people might just go out and do it in the storage room and then they don't care if you catch them or nothing like that.

Dora is young and one has the feeling that if the right time and place presented themselves, she would have no objections to doing it.

Friends

In these years friends are very important to both boys and girls, but a close friend is hard to cultivate in such a manipulative community, and very few girls keep the same close friends through high school.[6] Friends change schools, get pregnant, and/or get married, break your confidence, or start running with another crowd, and you drift apart from them. This happens with great regularity so that only one of the teenagers has managed to keep the same close friends through the teens—Christine Wards, who is still "tight" with Rosie Henry after over ten years. Glennora Patterson complains:

> Yeah, I had several friends, mostly girls. All of us was really tight. Three of them was older than I. You know, they graduated

[6] Seventy-four per cent of the persons with whom our respondents interacted most frequently were known less than eleven years, 49 per cent less than seven years, 24 per cent less than three years. In contrast, 9 per cent were non-relatives known since childhood. Stromberg, "A Preliminary Report . . . ," p. 74.

> before I did and graduated out of high school before I did too. One girl, me and her, we started grade school together. Now we're in the same grade. We stayed together. We went to the same school.
>
> *Q:* She's your close friend, is she?
>
> She used to be. . . . She can't help herself. She lies a great deal on people, you know.

Girlfriends do a lot of things together, mostly recreation after school: volleyball, dancing, joining various groups like singing groups. Double dating is not popular, parties are. One expects a great deal of one's close friends:

> They're my friends. . . . If I'm in need . . . if I really need something and they have it, I expect to be able to go to them and get it. And if they're my close friends, they wouldn't lie or nothing like that to me. . . . I wouldn't expect [them] to go with my boyfriend either.

Most of the time friends just get together and talk or listen to records. The conversation is mostly about boys, but strangely enough, "tight" friends are not likely to hear about such matters as a first pregnancy; such news is more frequently reported to a less well-known acquaintance. When a girl becomes pregnant, her old friends tend to drop away and she enters another circle—she is no longer a "school girl."

A lot of girls have boyfriends who are brothers of their girlfriends. Indeed, this is a common way in which couples meet. They are introduced by a sibling and, since many of these relationships result in children, families are interlocked by illegitimate children. This constitutes a kind of pseudo-kinship network that binds families together and offers some modicum of support.

In this community the word "girl" is a term of endearment when used between women, indicating a bond of solidarity and affection. It denotes "femininity" in a way for which there is no masculine counterpart. Quite often it is used in place of a first name. Thus, Mary tells of a conversation with a friend, "I said, 'You know if Karen wasn't a girl I'd go with her.' She said, 'Girl, you watch what you sayin', hear?' " When a mother scolds her daughter quite often it will be "Girl, don't you do that." She does not follow a comparable pattern for her sons.

Likewise, the use of the term "man" among men is too much associated with the reaction to Whitey's derogatory "boy" to be comparably used as a term of endearment among men. Furthermore, grown women in the project use the term "girl" in the same manner when referring to one another. "Woman" is rarely used. When it is, it generally means to be "somebody's woman." The term "man" is not extended downward to boys, and so a woman is a "girl" all of her life in a common bond of identity, but a boy becomes a man after he has proven himself—often by his sexual conquests.

THE GIRL'S VIEW OF MEN

The feminine attitude toward men is composed of a number of strands. A dominant element is disgust at their not being able to provide for their women.

Young Woman: What's wrong with these men today anyhow? They lazy. They don't wanna work. They get families, marry these girls . . . then they want to lay around.

Young Man: You know why . . . because they know if they try to get a job they couldn't get one.

Young Woman: I don't understand that. . . . I don't understand why it should be that way. I don't think it's actually that way, but most of the men are just like that.

Another element in their sentiment toward males is to be derived from their mother's account of her experience. Alliena Billit's mother gave her this advice:

"Alliena, let me tell you, *if you don't think you can just lay down and let that man walk all over you, don't you marry him.*" I thought that was so silly. I said, "Is that why you let daddy walk all over you?" She said, "I loved your daddy," as if I couldn't understand her saying that to me, but I do now. When her love was gone that was just it. She didn't take nothing off of him. I mean he would come in and say "Dee!" [Her father's nickname was "Bango."] She would say, "Call me by my name, right. Don't holler at me!" I can remember when this change came about and I would think,

> heck, maybe she's going to stand up for what's hers. By him beating on her so much, I swore I would never let a man beat me. And I don't.

Also among the attitudes that women have toward men is the notion that they think they are "too good" or too "uppity." Tilly, thirty-three exclaims:

> It seems like the men are wiser,[7] more intelligent, they think they know more. They think they do more and everything is just going too fast. . . . He probably knows more but probably thinks he knows double more and it just swells him and after a while that's a problem.

What is being said here is that the man knows more of the world of hard knocks, the street, and the world of wanderers. In Tilly's case, she was a high school dropout and, therefore, "average" in educational achievement.

The experience of boys "coming up" is the subject of the next chapter.

Conclusions

The data suggest the following generalizations:

1. Many lower-class Negro women who are first born daughters feel "overrun" with children both because of the extensive amount of time spent in their childhood caring for "her" (their mother's) children, and because of the large families of their own. They thus suppress an anger toward children that makes it difficult to discipline them because of the fear of "going too far." Indulgence toward children can be seen as one response to this inner anger.

2. Most ghetto adults, particularly women, admit to having more children than they desired.

3. Children pass out of the center of parental concern for a significant period in their grade school years. Formerly they were the center of attention and affection as the baby of the house, now they are comparatively ignored. Later they are once again much more central to

[7] Stromberg, *ibid.*, p. 20, indicates that men in the project have a slightly better median of years of education than the women (9.6 years to 8.7 years).

their parent's concern, but then it is more likely to be as sources of trouble (pregnancy, delinquency, etc.).

4. Sex is "natural" in the ghetto and girls generally "do it" to please their boyfriends. From an early age there is much experience in sexual play, but little understanding of the possible consequences. Some girls sometimes confess that they "did it" before they knew where babies came from.

5. For girls in their teens a choice must be made between planning a career (as typist, secretary, or nurse, for example) or "doing it" with their boyfriends. The decision to "do it" almost inevitably means pregnancy and the termination of their education. Not to "do it," however, means cutting oneself off from a central aspect of teenage life and an immediate mark of maturity (should a baby be born). The majority choose to "do it."

Chapter 3

Coming Up as a Boy in the Ghetto

While the feminine role is associated with respectability, dependability, the family, and the home, masculinity is more often associated with the reverse of these and its locus is the street. A boy strives to achieve a "rep" on the street because he perceives that he does not have much status in the home. He strives to assert his masculinity against almost overwhelming handicaps. His father still remembers his "place," but his mother is a recognized pillar of the family and the church and is the one who sees to it that he at least makes an effort in school. If he is in his late teens, he has seen in himself what he feared he saw all along in his father—a person ill-prepared to "go it alone." He sees himself more destined for the dependance of welfare than the independence of manhood. Coming up as a boy in the ghetto is thus a most difficult process indeed.

Boyhood and Blackness in Recollection

A part of the environment in which a boy becomes a man is his father's recollection of his own boyhood. Edward Patterson (forty-five) remembers his youth in Kentucky and southern Missouri:

> I mostly had a life of my own. . . . I traveled around quite a bit with my dad when I was a child. . . . From the time I can remember up until about twelve years old . . . [my father] was a fair speaking and understandable type of person. *He respected people and wanted to be respected. He more or less believed in minding his own affairs* and anything that didn't concern him, just wasn't any use for it. Definitely speaking, I believe that he

> thought like myself that it was a lot easier for him to get in other people's way than it was for them to get in his way because he was able to walk around [them] where the other person probably wouldn't agree to do such things.

Edward was a sickly child but helped out on the farm when he could. When he married, he farmed until he was twenty-four. In the back of his mind there was always the dream of owning a trailer and being able to travel so that he could "go where the work was available." His ideal was to have "a couple of kids"; he now has thirteen. His mother died when he was eleven, and his father took up with a girlfriend:

> It was a lady who lived nearby. [My older siblings] wouldn't agree to have another mother. . . . One could cook, the other could keep the house, . . . the two of us [boys] could bring enough in for us to have lunch and everything. So I guess we were just a very successful family.

When Edward was eighteen, his father died. Edward married when he was twenty-one, bringing to his marriage one illegitimate child, Herbert, whose mother had died in childbirth.

Arthur Washington (fifty-one) was born in Arkansas and moved into the boot-heel of Missouri as a young boy. His father was "a very industrious man" who sharecropped. "He was a good provider, a good church man, and was well liked by everyone." He died when Arthur was only sixteen. As he was coming up, Arthur had very little to do around the house. "The biggest we did was fish; we had no responsibility at all. Whatever my father said do, that's what we did."

A quite different boyhood is remembered by Stanley Billit (forty-four):

> I started plowing when I was eight . . . [with] horses and mules. . . . I could plow all day. [My father] was nothing but a farmer. He's still farming. He is a pretty good man. . . . Anybody could get along with him until he got mad. He'd just go crazy. . . . He could have five or six hundred dollars in his pocket and if you ask him for a dime, he'd swear he didn't have a dime.

Stanley didn't get very much schooling because he was always in the fields. He says that his father caught him playing hookey so much that he said: "Well, I'm just going to keep you to work since you don't want to go to school." Living in the city has convinced him that he ought to have gotten a better education, but now it is, as he sees it, too late for that. He left home when he was twenty-one to marry a girl from Mississippi. Both of his parents are still alive.

When he was nine, Andrew Buchanan (fifty-five) ran away from home. He lived by his "mother wit," sometimes visiting relatives, but often completely on his own. His father died shortly before he left home. Early life, for Andrew, was pretty much a matter of freewheeling, living off the land and the women encountered.

Andrew remembers his father:

> . . . mild, gentle, good—very good—just the type of a father a boy would want. Just one thing that was wrong with my father; he just wasn't home enough. . . . He worked in all types of capacities as a cook—that is, in hotels, restaurants, and even went on hunting parties with the hotel owner. He was a chief cook in a hotel. The owner of this hotel was going on a hunting trip and wanted him to go because he was also a barber and a good huntsman. I understand that he was a left-handed man and he shot very well. This seemed to be some kind of advantage because the people that he worked for never went on a hunting trip without taking him. Whenever they couldn't get a deer or bear, he did, and of course it was their bear. Not only that, he could cut their hair, shave them, all this kind of thing while he was on the hunting trip. It made him feel *almost essential to their hunting party.* This way he was away from home three to four weeks, a month at a time. Then they had boats and they had friends who had boats and they would go on excursions on the Mississippi on the *Kate Adams*—if I can remember right—in later years the *Jeff Hicks* . . . and daddy either cooked or waited tables on this party on these boats and he was away from home. Of course when he was home he seemed to me and my boyish ways to have plenty of money and was nice to me.

Andrew's own career reflects his father's. Once, while helping with a coat, he remarked: "I've had a lot of experience doing this. I'm pretty good as a shoeshine boy." He also followed up his father's interest in cooking, but not hunting.

Finally, Lester Frazier remembers his father, who was a sharecropper in Mississippi:

> [He] was a curious man. . . . He was good to his children and his wife. . . . Lots of men, they take the living out of the children's mouths and throw it away. . . . He worked the share because he wasn't able to afford to rent and take care of us.

Lester is particularly sensitive about his status as a Negro, and he makes explicit what is implied in all of the above remarks that speak of a father as a man who knows how to get along with people:

> I never did have no trouble out of white people. Didn't no white people ever beat on me or never cussed me. I always talked right to white people. I know how to treat anybody. I talked nice to them, I stayed in my place and wanted them to stay in their place. . . . Ain't none never attempted to hit me. The only thing is they just wouldn't pay me.

The components of masculinity revealed in these recollections of childhood indicate an early work orientation centering around the fields or unskilled labor on road gangs; or, as in Andrew's case, they reflect a father whose service was "almost essential" to his employer, who for all the world treated him as a slave "set free." They reflect a minimum of responsibility around the home. A boy's chores might be to bring in the wood for the fire and to milk the cows if there were any, but housework was women's work.

Lester could think of his father as peculiar because, in the experience of these men, it was not uncommon for a father to fail to care for his wife and children. It is perhaps significant that none of these men reports his own father as a derelict. Three of the five, however, lost their fathers before they were out of their teens. Combined with the enforced necessity of knowing one's place, the lack of an adequate male model undoubtedly contributed to their conception of handling situations passively by getting out of people's way or letting them run over you if need be.

While none of these men ever talked about their father "beating on" their mothers, several of the mothers who were described in the previous chapter stressed this fact about their fathers. A man frustrated in his relationship with the world outside his family takes it out on his wife and children, and this would seem to be quite often the case in project families.

These men, furthermore, are handicapped in teaching their sons a legitimate means of earning a living because the work that they did in the country is not available in the city or is of such low status that no young boy coming up would want "to be what his father was." They are also handicapped in helping their sons develop responsible behavior around the home as a direct consequence of this fact.

The problem of the Negro lower-class family—from the inevitably biased point of view of the dominant middle class—is, therefore, not so much a matter of the absence of a father as it is the absence of an *adequate* masculine role model *enabling adaptation* to the *values* of the larger culture. Most fathers do not seem to influence their sons significantly until the boy has begun to break away from the dominance of his mother and to move under the tutelage of his peers.

Babyhood and Boyhood in the Project

Freedom from Responsibility

As far as the three babies (one girl and two boys) born during the course of this study are concerned, no differential socialization by sex could be detected. As babies, boys and girls receive the same treatment. A great deal of affection and attention is given them until they begin to achieve some degree of autonomy. Then their siblings begin to lose interest in them. Babies are like dolls, things to play with and cuddle, but they soon become more trouble than they are worth. Only one child, the last child, can play the role of "family pet" for any length of time; the rest must quickly relinquish babyhood and the center of attention in the family world.

Birth order does not seem to be as important a factor affecting the early experience of boys as it does in the case of girls. Even the first-born boy is relieved of work around the house when he is living in the city. He must discover how a boy becomes a man outside of the family under the influence of his peers, while his sisters learn feminine roles close at home. Furthermore, mothers favor their girls more than their boys, both because of the girls' greater utility around the house and because men have numerous "pathologies" peculiar to their sex. A woman's experience of being exploited by men influences her attitude toward her sons.

Thus a boy must develop his sense of being a person and a man largely outside of the home and under the negative evaluation of his mother. He must further do this where the father is often missing or, if present, is likely to be preoccupied with the attempt to cover his own deep sense of failure with a facade of competence and rough hewn masculinity manifested in his physical, if not psychological, domination of his wife. Quite likely the male model provided by his father and older brothers is totally inadequate as a model for achieving mobility in the larger society. These older males may, on the other hand, be greatly admired as persons able to provide invaluable instruction in survival techniques for life in the ghetto. When this male role model is focused on his mother's boyfriend, the boy is made further aware of the possibilities of being a man without assuming full responsibility for a family. Some boyfriends, however, are amazingly competent as surrogate fathers.

The small boy in the project is made aware of his mother's preference for his sisters in numerous ways. Jerry Parvin, for example, knows this is true because his mother characteristically denies him the treats which she permits her daughters to have.

> *Jerry:* Can I have some can'y?
>
> *Lilly:* No!
>
> *Jerry* (whines and sulks around behind his mother pleading for some candy): Umm, Ummm, Canieeee, Ummm.
>
> [Jerry goes several times to the refrigerator, each time taking out the bag of candy and bringing it to his mother. Each time his mother refuses. He tries to ride a trike; she tells him to get off. Stephanie, his sister, watches with interest. She takes the trike away from Jerry and rides around the living room.]
>
> *Lilly:* I told you to put that trike in the closet. Did you hear me, Stephanie? Put that trike in the closet. You just riding it because you heard him say he wanted to. Neither of you can ride that trike.
>
> [Stephanie takes the trike and goes out into the hall. She rides

around a while then comes in and goes to the refrigerator, takes out the bag of orange slices, and gives some to a neighbor's child who has come into the apartment.]

Lilly: Come here, Stephanie Ann.

[Stephanie takes the bag of candy and gives some to all of the children present except Jerry. Jerry tries to take some candy himself.]

Lilly (shouting): Didn't I tell you not to get into that candy?

[Jerry stares hungrily at the candy. His mother goes out of the room for a few minutes. He takes a piece of candy and is chewing it when his mother comes back into the room. Lilly makes no comment although she has seen that he has taken a piece.]

In this instance Lilly's official permission was denied to both Jerry and his sister, but from past experience Stephanie knows that she can get away with such activities in open defiance of her mother's wishes. Jerry, if he is to be successful, must do it behind his mother's back. Stephanie enjoys such a privileged position in her family because she is a girl, and although only ten, she takes a great deal of the work that is done around the house off her mother's hands. Jerry does nothing, is not required to do anything, and is treated accordingly.

Lilly also sees in Jerry his father's evils. At the age of nine he is, in his mother's eyes, already a little man who must be prevented from stepping into his father's shoes. On another occasion Jerry was aggressively acting out an attempted robbery which he claimed actually happened to the Parvin family. He kicked and shouted at the unseen assailant and then, exhausted, sat down to put on a pair of oversize shoes. His sister shouted a warning: "Them's men's shoes, them's men's shoes," and looked sheepishly at her mother when asked to explain. Her mother volunteered: "She means them shoes too big for Jerry. He's trying to be a little man now. He thinks he is a man." That this fact has highly symbolic overtones for Lilly was revealed a bit later when she remarked:

Jerry, he don't want to mind at all. I try to send him to the store with Stephanie and them so he can get some fresh air sometimes, and he don't want to go. A man told me he's watching me. . . . Somebody put Jerry up to watching me. . . . Anyway, I

Table III AVERAGE AGE AT WHICH RESPONDENTS THINK PROJECT YOUTH (UNDER AGE 25) BEGIN VARIOUS ACTIVITIES*

Activity	Boys (*Per Cent*†)						Girls (*Per Cent*†)					
	Ave. Age	−2 yr.	−1 yr.	Ave.	+1 yr.	+2 yr.	Ave. Age	−2 yr.	−1 yr.	Ave.	+1 yr.	+2 yr.
Dropped a bottle out of window on concrete below	7.8	13.3	13.3	13.7	7.9	11.5	8.5	10.0	12.8	9.5	10.9	14.7
Stole something from a store	8.9	7.1	11.2	8.0	17.4	15.6	10.9	5.9	10.9	13.6	5.9	12.7
Knew how to jive, play the dirty dozens	10.8	8.0	6.2	13.3	6.2	14.2	11.5	3.6	12.6	4.9	16.6	8.1
Danced with a girl (boy)	11.2	5.6	12.2	8.7	23.5	12.2	11.5	1.3	8.3	10.5	23.6	17.8
Played hookey from school for two or three days at a time	11.7	7.5	14.9	7.0	16.7	11.4	12.9	11.7	3.2	19.4	15.3	18.0
Kissed and felt up a girl (kissed and was felt up by a boy)	12.9	7.9	5.7	22.0	14.5	16.3	12.8	9.3	12.0	20.4	12.8	12.4
Smoked cigarettes fairly often	12.7	9.5	6.9	17.7	12.5	19.4	13.4	6.1	18.2	18.2	22.1	15.6
Had sexual relations with a girl or woman (boy or man)	14.2	9.8	13.0	20.1	25.0	17.0	13.8	4.0	15.1	18.7	17.8	23.1
Drank enough wine, beer, or whiskey to get high	14.2	10.0	11.8	21.8	22.7	15.3	15.1	9.3	18.6	18.6	23.4	11.1
Got into a fight in which someone was badly hurt	14.8	8.8	9.7	15.4	19.3	18.9	14.5	8.5	11.7	17.9	19.3	17.9
Made a girl pregnant (got pregnant)	15.6	5.8	13.3	25.3	23.1	22.2	14.2	8.8	24.7	24.2	21.2	14.9
Smoked marihuana	15.6	7.9	9.4	18.3	21.8	17.8	15.9	8.0	14.6	13.7	21.1	15.6
Had homosexual relations with a girl or woman (boy or man)	15.7	6.1	9.7	14.6	16.4	5.5	16.2	10.2	10.8	15.6	6.6	25.2

* This is a modified version of the data presented in Stromberg, "Perspectives on Pathology . . .," p. 27.

† Percentages are calculated for each full year. Thus if the average age is 7.8, 13.7 per cent of the respondents felt the average age was between 7 & 7.9 years & 7.9 per cent felt it was between 8 & 8.9 years (listed under +1).

been trying to get him out of here because I think you should play like little kids should play.

Q: Why would Jerry be watching you?

I don't know. I know I don't have a husband or nothing. . . . I think that kinda keeps me upset. . . . One day I was getting ready to go to the store and he began aggravating me and getting on my nerves. . . . I went over there to the door and he start talking like he been planning something.

In her illness Lilly exaggerates sentiments held by other mothers in the project to the point where she imagines that her son is a potential rapist. She further projects the responsibility for all of the evils she observes in him on various male relatives. His uncle taught him homosexual play; his father is responsible for his aggressiveness. Jerry Parvin's case is the case of every boy in the project writ large and explicit, rather than covertly expressed in subtle preferences and avoidances.

Breaking Away from Mother: The Dozens

The masculine struggle against the feminine domination of the "stable," respectable world of the family is dramatized most clearly in the custom of "playing the dozens." Project residents believe that boys begin to play the dozens when they are about eleven years old and girls when they are about a half year older (Table III). While the game is played by both boys and girls, it is preeminently a male activity in which the mother is made the target of ridicule and satire.[1] Even when girls play, the imagery retains an assertion of masculine virility, as evidenced by this rhyme given by a six-year-old girl:

I was walking through the jungle
With my dick in my hand
I was the baddest motherfucker
In the jungle land.
I looked up in the tree
And what did I see
Your little black mama

[1] John Dollard, "The Dozens: The Dialect of Insult," *American Imago*, I (1939), 3–24.

Trying to piss on me.
I picked up a rock
And hit her in the cock
And knocked that bitch
A half a block.[2]

Abrahams notes that in his experience "one occasionally finds girls making dozen-type remarks, but for the most part not in the organized fashion of the boys."[3] One function of the dozens common to both sexes is the training in verbal ability which is a necessary part of the male-female interchange of the late teens and early adulthood.

For the boy entering puberty, however, the dozens has a very specific function. It enables him to break free from the world of the mother and enter the world of the man, expressed in its earliest form in the project as the "gang."

In playing the dozens the boy can subject the mother, who is the chief dispenser of love and care, as well as discipline and authority, to criticism and abuse within the confines of a rigidly defined rhythmic game which prevents the volatile activity from getting out of hand. Playing the dozens occurs at the point when the boy is about to enter puberty and suffer his greatest rejection from his mother as a result of his becoming a man. The dozens enables him to develop a defense against this rejection and provides a vehicle for his transition into the manipulative world of the street dominated by masculine values expressed in gang life. By the end of adolescence the incipient mistrust between the sexes becomes an overt and central aspect of a way of life for both men and women. The dozens is thus a "ritualized exorcism" enabling the combatants to break away from the family dominated by the mother and to establish their own image of male superiority celebrated in street life.[4]

The dozens also functions to inform both sexes of some of the aspects of sexuality at an early age. These verbal contests acquaint children with many details of sexuality, often before they are otherwise aware of them. They are a kind of primer imparting information about the sex act, sexual deviance, sexual anatomy, and mores which

[2] Boone Hammond, "The Contest System: A Survival Technique" (St. Louis: Washington University Essay Series in Sociology, December 1965), p. 23.

[3] Roger D. Abrahams, "Playing the Dozens," *Journal of American Folklore,* LXXV (July 1962), 207–20.

[4] *Ibid.,* p. 214.

serves as basic guidelines for children who are exposed to sexuality early and completely without being reared in a home where the matters of sex are commonly talked about.

The Perceived Trajectory of Boyhood: Problems and Privileges

Boys become problems at an earlier age than girls in the eyes of project residents (Table III). They are more difficult to manage, engage in such activities as dropping bottles out of windows (sometimes aimed at persons below), stealing, playing hookey from school, smoking cigarettes, drinking to get drunk, smoking marihuana, and engaging in homosexual activities at an earlier age than girls. They are not seen, however, as engaging in most heterosexual activities at an earlier age. Girls and boys begin dancing and kissing at about the same age, but girls experience the sex act at an earlier age and consequently become pregnant earlier than boys engage in sex and become responsible for making a girl pregnant.

Boys demonstrate their lack of fear and begin to cultivate their aggressiveness in such activities as dropping objects on people from the gallery windows and stealing small objects from the store. Often the items a boy steals are not used or sold. They are stolen "just for kicks." A girl, on the other hand, begins to steal later because she steals items she uses, such as clothing and make-up. These become important to her when she begins to consider her chances with the other sex.

However, the activities engaged in by both sexes before the age of fourteen—or about the time most project youngsters are getting out of grade school—are not activities that are going to get them into much trouble with "the man," nor bring much trouble into the home. The objects stolen in the early years are usually small and can be returned or paid for if the child is caught. Trouble comes in midteens, and then it often comes as a surprise, even though the child has been gradually developing a deviant career for almost seven years.[5]

[5] Howard Becker's concept of a deviant career and the importance of "labeling" as marking a significant turning point in that career is highly relevant here. Howard Becker, *The Outsiders: Studies in the Sociology of Deviance* (New York: The Macmillan Company, 1966), pp. 25 ff.

The likelihood of a boy being labeled as a deviant while he is in his teens is thus great.[6] This label, however, in the ghetto becomes not a mark of rebuke but a medal and a further indication of having a "rep." Police records, plus the prized ability to "make out," are at one and the same time rejections of the values of the white world from which one is barred by virtue of race, and the respectable home from which one is barred by feminine values enforced by a rejecting mother and taunting sisters. A boy has no other choice in his struggle to become a man than to reject the home or conform to feminine and/or white values. He achieves his identity, therefore, as a Negro and as a man in the street by earning a "rep" because he has not been able to develop an identity as a respected member of his household.

Not all boys follow this deviant trajectory, but a significant number—perhaps a majority—do. In the group of teenagers in these families, only one, possibly two, boys (Richard Frazier and Jeremiah Brown) seem to be consistently following a "more acceptable" line of development, earning their spending money at odd jobs and preferring their own company to that of their peers. Even they, however, ran with a "gang" for a while before deciding that they did not want to "run with people who had trouble on their minds."

Gangs and Running Buddies

Although the gang in the classical sense is not a part of boyhood in the project, informal groups which are called "gangs" are. These gangs are rarely given names, they do not have emblems on their backs, or formal structures, though they usually have recognized leaders and may dress alike to the extent that all will wear a particular style of hat. Nicknames like "Daddio," "Big Pops," and "Coco" serve to identify a close relationship among members, or to define a significant aspect of a member's personality. The gang is usually a group of from seven to fifteen boys in their early to mid-teens who hang around together for a summer or two and whose apparent main objectives are stealing and fighting.

Richard Frazier (fifteen) gives this account of his experience:

> I know when I was running with a gang about thirteen of us

[6] In this group of teenagers, 61 per cent of the boys have police records, 29 per cent of the girls, or 48 per cent of the total teenage population.

> were together and with me it was fourteen. They was going to steal something. They said, "Man, we're going to make him [Richard] go in there and get it." I said, "Naw you ain't going to make me go there 'cause I'm fixing to go. . . . This is my last night with you." They said, "It don't make us no difference. We should make you go in there and get it anyway." After I saw them getting in trouble, I just came on back. . . . I don't follow people that have trouble on their minds.

Boys more than girls are under the influence of their peer group when coming up, and the tendency of this influence is to foster deviant behavior. If a boy is going to get into trouble, project residents believe that he will get into quite a few "serious troubles" by the time he is sixteen. Robbing, stealing, drinking, teenage fighting, promiscuity, and having children before marriage are seen as both serious and frequent troubles.[7] The joy ride, drinking party, "gang bang," and purse snatching episodes are quite often part of the activities of these gangs.

Gangs, like friends, however, do not stay together very long. The membership changes, gets older, ends up in reform school, or simply loses interest in running with each other, and so the gang disbands. Gerald Buchanan claims that in the early sixties there were several large gangs in the project, but these disbanded when their leaders were "sent up." When they disbanded, no organized group replaced them, but project boys still hang around together and seek their kicks where they can find them.

Another group that is characteristic of the teenage boy is the singing group. The fields of entertainment and athletics have thus far offered the most conspicuous avenues for upward mobility for Negro ghetto youth. One very apparent indicator of the extent to which these youth desire mobility is the number of teenagers in the project who train for these fields. Many never reach an audition or a tryout, but the effort they exert as amateurs testifies to their not having opted out of the struggle for success.

Four or five boys and occasionally a girl or two will get together quite regularly and practice. One group, the Mellmonts, sings in apart-

[7] Jerome Stromberg, "Perspectives on Pathology, Socialization, Religion and World View of Project Residents," p. 10.

ments, downstairs janitors' rooms, or anywhere it can gather an audience. The songs sung are about the problems of love, the hardships of life, and occasionally a bit of the blues, although the blues are generally recognized as a sign of both "old age" and a rural background. Most teenagers here, as everywhere, prefer rock and roll. Disappointment in love is the most common theme:

> Two stupid feet set down beside you
> You wring my heart in two
> But till they discover
> You really love another
> Two stupid feet walk back to you.

Because large groups of any character tend to be undependable, a boy seeks a close running buddy to help him in his fighting and help him out in life's troubles. These dyadic relationships tend to be more stable than larger ones, but even they are not of long duration because the expectations boys have of a running buddy are usually beyond his ability to fulfill. A buddy doesn't have the money you need when you need it; he is almost as prone to steal your girl as any one else, and when it comes right down to it, he doesn't trust you any more than you really trust him. All relationships with one's peers, therefore, are tenuous, and the boy in his late teens, while he may have one or more running buddies, is generally prepared to face life on its own terms alone. Hammond writes:

> "Go for yourself" means in a sense do what you're big enough to do because you are the one who must suffer the consequences in a culture that says you can do as much "wrong" as you like, but shame on you if you get caught. In this setting, limits are where the individual doers put them. What would be considered in middle-class terms as deviant behavior is highly tolerated.[8]

Gerald's Perspective

Gerald Buchanan was fifteen when the study began. The problems of teenage boys are well presented in his career. From this one teenager's point of view, many things are "natural" that might, from a middle-class point of view, be considered deviant. Thus there is the matter of vandalism:

[8] Hammond, *op. cit.*, p. 9.

> You know kids. They used to be real high fences and then they cut them down, half size. And that did it. The kids got tired of walking around. They would kick one of em loose and just start throwing it, doing everything. . . . I can't feel too bad about this because I do it myself. I don't feel too bad about it. I feel neutral about it.

And of course sexual intercourse is considered natural even for a thirteen-year-old. Gerald was once asked, "How do you view girls that get pregnant at thirteen?" He replied:

> I think of them the same way I thought of them before they were pregnant 'cause myself, I like to get a little just like the next one. I think the fella's usually in a mess because he ain't got no job and he can't support her. So the mother usually have to take care of the girl. And she did it once . . . well she'll be the wiser.

Part of the problem of adolescence is running with the wrong crowd. There are so many temptations in this environment and so many kids on the loose that it is difficult not to run with the wrong crowd. Gerald was asked if he ever belonged to a gang and he replied much like Richard Frazier (see pp. 70–71):

> Ah, I used to be with them say a lot. I used to be with them, but I never did when they go to steal something. I go home . . . [and] they start telling some other of their friends about Gerald, "Gerald ain't nothing, man, that nigger scared. We got ready to go steal some money over on Newberry. He wouldn't even go with us." I wasn't interested, so they passed the word and I got popular by being unpopular with them.

Thus Gerald does not consider himself to be one of the "thuggish" crowd. But he has been in constant contact with the police nevertheless.

He has been taken down to police headquarters on several occasions. He brags, "I been to Ram Street once, I been to Ninth, I been to Eight, Gotham. . . . I got tooken down the Eighth District for curfews [being out after 1:00]." He also has made many trips to Central. Gerald claims, however, that he has never been convicted.

His exploits seem to be pretty typical of boys in the project. For example:

> There was a laundry truck down there in front of Opal's home and me and my buddy were snatching clothes out of it and we started running. There was a police car right around there talking to a project policeman named M. . . . They were over there. [They] took out their gun and thought maybe they were going to shoot somebody so I stopped. So M., he calls you "little punk," . . . he choked me and then he told me [them] "Take this little punk and get on down" and then I got in the car and they took me down there [Main]. The one that took me down, he was nice. He was going to let me go, but seeing that I been down there before he didn't let me go, so I stayed four hours.

He also tells of another run-in with the police:

> One day me and a boy named Ike, we were downtown. I didn't go downtown with him. I saw him down there. He was stealing stuff, and a boy named Arthur he was with him, and they left outside the building. The man brought in a shipment of Knoxs, and set it outside the building and Arthur grabbed a box and I grabbed a box and so they caught me, but he got away. They took me over to Central District, and you know, they will try to make you tell a lie. They say I went down there with him . . . that I purposely came down there to see him. That wasn't it at all. Since I saw a chance like that I went and took it. If they think you lying and you keep on sticking to what you saying, they get mad and hit you.

Thus stealing, like other deviant behavior, is very much a part of the teenager's way of life, although in general more rationalization is required to justify such activity. Gerald himself has a record of four arrests for petty theft and joyriding.

The conviction that one is going to end up in jail is neither uncommon nor unrealistic. One of Gerald's running buddies, Samuel, was asked, "What do you think will happen to you?" and he replied, "I'll end up in the pen somewhere." "What makes you think that?" "Sometimes I be thinking that. . . . My mother always talking, she say, 'You need to be put somewhere where you can stay out of trouble.'" Sam was sentenced to nine months in the State Reformatory for Boys in the summer of 1965 for his part in an armed robbery where another boy was knifed. He took part in a riot in the Reformatory and was sentenced to six months more and thus is still in detention.

From Gerald's point of view his mother is his biggest problem as a teenager because she constantly tries to "mother" him. "She tries to kiss me and do all that before you go anywhere." He handles this by provoking her to anger:

> I joke with her. She tell me, "Mind your manner." I say, "Aw shut up." I be playing with her and stuff like that. I don't mean it. I aggravate her, you know, trying to get her back out of here. I aggravate her again. She say she going to hit me, but she never do.

And so he won't ask his mother for money, but rather turns to his father who also gives him an understanding ear:

> He understands you. He used to tell me he had the same trouble most every trouble I have had, he'd have so you know when he was small. He said, I dealing with it all right. Therefore I come to him a whole lot.
>
> *Q:* Do you think he's a special father?
>
> Well, used to be, but not any more. You know, I told him I want to learn to drive and he ain't got round to it yet. I'm kinda mad at him.

At the end of the study Gerald was nineteen, a high school graduate by virtue of the equivalency exam, unemployed, separated from a wife and two children, and unable to join the Air Force because of his police record. He has thus experienced frustration, failure, and fatherhood before he has come of age.

Early Attempts at Earning Money Legitimately

While the boy is not expected to do much work around the house, there is some expectation that he will at least make the effort to find part-time work. Most boys in their teens have done some work for pay, though the majority do not have regular part-time jobs. Richard Frazier (fifteen) has the most regular work history of the younger boys, having held a job in a grocery store as a carry out clerk for several months. T. J. Patterson (nineteen), a high school graduate, has perhaps made the best job adjustment of the older boys, although he is at present out of a job. He worked for a local packing company for about a year and for a nearby refrigerator company for a few weeks. In both he performed only manual work. Although he is the only member of his family to finish high school, present job opportunities look no better for him than they do for his other siblings, so he is taking night school courses and trying to improve his education. He remains hopeful that his education will eventually improve his job opportunities. Gerald Buchanan has had numerous jobs, including helping clean up the project through the Youth Corps, working in the local assembly plant, and taking training under programs offered in the Job Corps. He has not stayed more than a few weeks at any one job. He works until he gets a couple of pay checks and then lays off to play pool (to the consternation of his parents). Gerald has found his high school equivalency diploma to be useless in getting him the job he wants. The Washington boys, Levan (nineteen), Jerry (sixteen), Lee (eighteen), and Howard (fifteen), have helped their father out on his truck, and have also been employed in several part-time jobs outside the family. (Only one of eight teenage daughters, Barbara Wards, is presently working, and in fact she has been working regularly at a local department store for almost two years.)

Most boys have a fuzzy notion about what they want to be, or else they want to be like someone they see regularly and who, they fancy, must live an exciting existence. For example, Richard claims, along with Sam, that he wants to be a policeman.[9] Gerald has aspirations of being an electrical engineer, by which he means someone who repairs appliances or airplanes, whichever he can find training to become. Several of the boys find the Army a way out of their job problems. James Perry (seventeen) and Nathan Patterson are now in the service. As we have seen, Gerald tried to get into the Air Force, but

[9] The implications of this fact are more fully explored in David A. Schulz, "Some Aspects of the Policeman's Role as It Impinges Upon the Lower-Class Negro Family" (Paper presented to the American Sociological Association, Boston, August 1968).

his police record kept him out. He has not applied for induction into the Army. By and large the services are not very attractive to the boys in the project.

Richard Frazier

For the boy who has recently moved to the city, the contrast between the expectations of his parents and what he is able to provide in the way of help is often a source of conflict. This is best exemplified in the case of Richard Frazier. He is quite a contrast to his parents. While they are of the country, he has quickly picked up city ways. At fifteen he is a sharp dresser from his Knox hat to his highly polished shoes. Richard remembers Mississippi somewhat differently than his parents, who tend to romanticize it:

> You have to pick cotton down there but up here you know it's different. . . . You don't have to do up here as you do down there because [there] you come back out of the field [and cook lunch or dinner and go right back out in the field] . . . [and the] stores down there are different to me. . . . Shoes down there and up here look like to me they're two different pairs. . . . You can get better shoes up here.

The city has meant freedom from field work and chores, as well as access to things like new clothes and many new acquaintances. His father stands with the comfortable casualness of a farm hand, whereas Richard stands tall, pulls precisely at a cigarette, and looks you over with the air of deceptive confidence characteristic of the street. He is often to be found slouching teenage fashion in the living room club chair, talking to friends on the phone. His father does not feel at ease talking over a phone.

Having already acquired more than three times the formal education of either of his parents by virtue of being a sophomore in high school, he is often called upon to carry out the necessary family business. Bills from creditors, doctor's prescriptions, instructions from government agencies like Welfare pass through his hands. He is especially useful in answering the many notes from the school regarding himself and his brothers and sisters. For a while he had managed to convince his parents that he was going to graduate this year, but they discovered their error and are trying to convince him that he ought to stay in school until he finishes high school. He decided, finally, to complete school.

Richard thus has a certain status in the family by virtue of being such an important link with the outside world. His younger sister Rosie Joe shares some of this, but she is much more reticent and less well prepared to handle such important matters. It is not an easy thing for his parents to accept their dependence upon him, a dependence that they probably would not have felt as acutely if they were still living in the country.

THE STRATEGY OF COOL[10]

Playing it cool is an important aspect of what Rainwater has called "the expressive life style." [11] This survival technique is an attempt to "make yourself interesting and attractive to others so that you are better able to manipulate their behavior along lines that will provide some immediate gratification." [12] When a person "loses his cool," he has become victimized by this strategy or "put in a trick." Playing it cool is thus a defense against exploitation.

Learning to lie effectively is central to the notion of "cool" and the expressive life style. Children are taught early that it does not pay to tell the truth, particularly to strangers who might be bill collectors, plain clothes "fuzz," or simply someone interested in some personal and immediate gratification. The following is an attempted deception undertaken by two eight-year-olds:

> Annette then went over to the window in the living room and put her hand behind the curtain and was looking out. She put

[10] The following definition of cool is offered by Robert H. DeCoy in his *The Nigger Bible* (Los Angeles: Holloway House Publishing Co., 1967), p. 30: "Cool, n.v.—In control, wise, aloof, detached. A state of being in admirable possession of one's wit and emotions."

[11] Lee Rainwater, "Work and Identity in the Lower Class," in *Planning for a Nation of Cities,* ed. Sam H. Warner (Cambridge: M.I.T. Press, 1967). For a succinct picture of street life, see John Horton, "Time and Colored People," *Trans-action,* IV (April 1967), 5–12.

[12] Lee Rainwater, "Crucible of Identity: The Negro Lower-Class Family," *Daedalus,* XCV (Winter, 1966), 206.

her hand behind her and turned to me and said: "I lost my quarter."

"How did you do that?"

"It fell out the window. Give me another one."

"No! I don't have another one to give you."

"But mine's gone."

Clinton then went over to where she was and said: "No you didn't; you still got it."

Annette grinned and reached behind the curtain and opened her hand and brought it back and said, "See, I found my quarter."

Clinton tried the same thing and said: "I lost my nickel."

"Did you? What happened?"

"It fell."

Annette said: "You didn't lose it either."

Clinton then came over to where I was and pushed his quarter underneath a stand and said: "I lose mine. Give me another." [13]

What appears to be an impossible deception to an outside observer is not considered as such by Clinton, who has seen equally obvious lies frequently rewarded. This is especially true in the small matter of begging for pennies—a constant activity of the children in the project. Sometimes the necessity for giving the gift is implied in the situation with a stranger, who ought to be able to perceive that you are poor and therefore in need. Often the encounter is simply initiated: "Give me a penny." One young ten-year-old boy was asked in return, "Why, do many people give you pennies?" His reply was: "Yes, because I do things for them." This he said while dancing away chanting: "Wash the car, clean out the garage . . . ," knowing full well that what he was saying was untrue and that he was begging for pennies without ever having done anything to earn what he received. In this situation, however, he was unable to continue the pretense and made as graceful an exit as he could.

Another important function of the lie in the ghetto is "face saving." The Cadillac, the forty-five dollar shoes, the one hundred and twenty

[13] These notes on the Buchanan family were made by a colleague, Miss Gwendolyn Jones.

dollar suit tell the world, "I'm a success and I've been around," although the reality is ordinarily quite grim. Gerald Buchanan carried this off quite well in a small way when he remarked at a restaurant that he had tasted all of the twelve or thirteen wines on the wine list except the ruby port which he selected.

This need to create a world with the appearance of success and personal competence has interesting repercussions. On one occasion Mrs. Buchanan claimed, "Gerald is in Indiana. He's in Job Corps training now," despite the fact that he was at the time in the bedroom and soon came out to say hello. For her son to have been in Indiana was very important to Betty Re because it marked for her the beginning of his assuming responsibility for his wife and children. In this instance the word "lie" is perhaps not quite accurate to describe what took place, as it may well have been an expression of a deep wish fervently believed in and not an intentional deception.

The hustler is the epitome of this phenomenon and an idol of the "cool" world. The hustler is aware of his front, but in less stressful situations a man of the ghetto may well assume a front and afterward come to believe in it, not as a game, but as a part of himself.

Working Game

The manipulative, aggressive aspect of "cool" is seen in working game. The verbal dexterity required for working game is developed in playing the dozens. Several teenage boys constantly worked the author for small change while he was in the project, and they always had a ready reason for needing the money. They needed "carfare to get to grandfather's house" or to the "draft board" or "to look for a job" or to "buy lunch," usually adding that if they didn't get what they needed, something serious would happen to them. They begged money on the pretense of needing food only a few times, but when they were successful, they often turned it into wine or beer.

The following gives an example of their game:

Gerald: Give me a quarter.

Interviewer: Why?

G: Well, see, I gotta go to work tomorrow, and I don't have carfare.

I: Did you get a job?

G: Yeah, I got a job on Middlebury and Park.

I: Doing what?

G: Well, washing woodwork and things.

I: How much do you get paid?

G: Forty-five dollars a week.

I: How long do you have to work for that?

G: From nine until four-thirty.

I: How did you get the job?

G: Well, a man in the building, on the elevator that I know, he talking about it one night and he works out there and he got me a job.

[At this point the interviewer decided to give Gerald the quarter for the heck of it and tossed it to him.]

Sam: I need a quarter too.

I: Why do you need a quarter?

S: I ain't got nothing to eat.

G: You can see what he's trying to eat can't ya [boiled egg sandwich]?

I: How is it that you don't have anything to eat at this time of day?

S: Well, my mother left and she went to work and she didn't leave any money in the house and I don't have anything to get lunch with.

I: Aw come on now Sam; you can do better than that.

S: No, honest, that's the truth, ain't it, Gerald?

G: Sure is.

The author gave Sam a quarter; they took their money and left, presumably to buy food. The author stayed behind with Mary, Gerald's girlfriend, assuring them he would remain only a few minutes. In about fifteen minutes they returned with a bag and went into the bedroom. Mary said that Gerald "is embarrassed to eat in front of people, so he's gonna eat in the bedroom."

Feeling that he knew the boys well enough, the author decided to visit them in the bedroom where he found them drinking beer and wine. They were totally unmoved at being unmasked, for by their teens they had been well trained in playing it cool.

The author asked, "Why didn't you tell me that you wanted to buy some beer?" He had done this several times for them in the past. Gerald replied: "Because we didn't think you'd give us the money." Of course, Gerald did not have a job at all, but since the author was interested in his getting a job, he frequently used this as a cover to hide his real intentions when he did not want to be bothered by the author, or when he wanted something from him. In contrast to the example of Annette and Clinton, Mary and Sam decided to support Gerald in his deception. Thus the maintenance of a lie often becomes a group activity that may well pay off to more than one member.

While this example could be interpreted merely as the common mode of treatment given to white outsiders, it is also a very common form of interaction between members themselves. This is particularly true in rapping or jiving a girl in order to obtain her sexual favors.[14] Sometimes the manipulation of the other is carried out with a minimum of verbal interaction. Thus Mr. Buchanan frequently obtains small change from friends by pocketing change for drinks when the friends are too drunk to know the difference.

The Pimp

In the cool world the ideal relationship (from the young male's point of view) between the sexes is achieved by the man who "pimps" a woman.[15] In this type of relationship the woman supports the man. In the classic understanding of the term, a pimp may live off the labors of several prostitutes, getting a stylish living in return for services such as protection, banking for jail bond and saving purposes, and "fix" procurement in the case of legal action. This type is still prevalent. Thus Sam tells of his friend who has diamond rings and Cadillacs derived from the income of five prostitutes who live with

[14] Greater detail is to be found in Hammond, *op. cit.*, pp. 35–42.

[15] The more general term covering the situation where a woman supports a man is not acceptable usage to a professional pimp, who calls these persons "studs" and claims they have no expertise or professional skills.

him and his wife and children, but conduct their business elsewhere. Andrew Buchanan (fifty-five) confides that for about three years he enjoyed the life of a pimp as a young man and remembers that he always had several hundred dollars in his pocket and always dressed in the best of style:

> Due to the time, the economics of the time . . . I didn't have no money. If you found a girl who had a nice big house (they had seven or eight other girls in there), maybe she was working, maybe her old man was a chauffeur for the same family, had a whole lot of income coming. You wouldn't have to worry about a place to stay and no food or clothes. And if you was diligent enough you could have some money. These girls made fifteen or twenty dollars a night. [They] didn't do a thing but drink it up and buy some stockings. I didn't drink so I could stash some money and it kept me with a nice bankroll when I got situated. I could go around and play a little policy, do some cheap gambling, have a suit on every day, have a cigar and be dressed up. Kept forty, fifty dollars all the time. After becoming acquainted with these girls, I guess my very character and the way I carried myself, they trusted me. So, therefore, all the money they had left, maybe one dollar, maybe fifty cents, they would give to me for the bank. So that made me a big bankroll—a hundred dollars or so in my pocket. Say there came a girl, some kind of saintly too, some had families they had to support, they would like to save their money until Friday or Saturday. They tell their mama they been working (they should have been going to school). I would give them their money, which was minus fifty cents or a dollar. Then some of them (the older ones didn't have anybody to give any money to particularly) they save their money for the time they might get arrested. At that time about fifteen dollars would take them down to court, and if they would go into the workhouse, fifteen dollars would take them out. So they would save money.

However, the term also covers the more general situation where a man lives off a woman who is not a prostitute and who earns her living legitimately as a professional, a well-paid clerk or domestic, or a welfare recipient. Hence, the excitement of "Mother's Day," the tenth of the month when the welfare checks come in the mail and "the eagle flies." Pimping seems to be the younger man's approach to the dilemma of poverty, low status in the larger culture, and unemployment. In the language of the street, a "cat" is usually a pimp. Thus Mary (eighteen) says that a "cat" can:

> . . . be a girl or a boy and they wants to be cool, wants to be hip, jive, you know. If it's a boy, he try to pimp off a woman. He going to lovey dovey up on her . . . if she got some money . . . they gonna use their power to get the money from you. . . . You know, like telling the girl that she got "Cleopatra eyes" and that she be "sweeter than a cherry." . . . She probably buy him clothes and he ain't giving her nothing but a little love and stuff like that. . . . For instance a lot of these cats gets a woman about thirty-nine or something and she not married and do have a good job.

The role of the pimp, then, is most characteristically that of a young man seeking an older woman who may have a comfortable income and feels that her powers of attraction are fading. Sam explains the willingness of a woman to "pimp a man" under the rubric of "she loves him." Love, for Sam, implies a willingness to do anything for the person who is loved, including "bringing them their slippers, lighting their cigarettes. . . . Man, if a woman loves you, you got it made, there ain't nothing you have to do . . . you don't have to lift your little finger."

This conception of love is in keeping with a general tendency to demand evidence of concern, even, as here, to the point of exploitation in the small matters of everyday life. Irvin (seventeen) explains the problems of city life in terms of a declining emphasis upon concrete and traditional expressions of love. He believes that kids are so bad these days because they are raised on cow's milk rather than their mother's milk; they have been placed more often in the hands of baby-sitters, and as infants no longer receive their food premasticated from their mother's mouth. The pimp takes advantage of this need to concretize relationships. He constantly demands that his woman demonstrate her affection by providing him with a high standard of living (by ghetto standards) while he demonstrates his by his capacity as a lover.

Mary Perry maintains that she knows a boy "who is nineteen years old and he got a woman [thirty-nine] 'up tight.' . . . She's a nurse and she gets paid every month . . . and he gets just about half of her check and comes and spends it on us." The final insult of the pimp—and the fear of any woman keeping one—is that he will take her money and spend it on other women, demonstrating that despite her care for him, he cares not a whit for her. The pimp is, in some sense, the urban counterpart of the relationships between rural woman and the wandering men who moved from lumber camp to lumber camp living off the women they could find in each. There the exchange, however, was rarely of money, but rather an exchange of intimacies.

"Pimping" is but one of several non-marital roles a man can play. He can in certain unusual situations take full advantage of a woman's holdings and exploit her with even less reciprocity. Thus Lilly Parvin claims Ronnie tries to rape her occasionally and sometimes succeeds. Other relationships that indicate a greater degree of commitment and reciprocity on the part of the male will be discussed under the role of the boyfriend in the next chapter.

Learning "Cool"

"Playing it cool" is thus primarily the way of the street, but it extends into the family as well and results in some painful paradoxes. If the mother is to train her child for survival on the street, she must train him in the arts of manipulation and deception. The following is an excellent account of the process by which a young boy is ushered into the cool world by his mother:

> Darryl, age seven, tells his mother that he needs a quarter so he can attend the movies in school. Mary, his sister, age eight, then tells her mother not to listen to him because he is lying so he can have the money for himself. She goes to the same school and she assures her mother that no money is necessary to see the movies. Darryl stands quietly with a sheepish grin on his face. His mother asks if he really needs money. Darryl says very meekly that he does. Mary shouts: "No he doesn't; he's lying."
>
> His mother practically shouts back: "DARRYL BE A MAN! Speak up for yourself, boy."

> It was obvious from the expression on Darryl's face that he was lying—that fact seemed to be understood by everyone. His mother asks him again if he needs the money. This time a little louder, still not very manly, he says: "I sure do," and now he adds a few embellishments. "My teacher told me to bring the money, 'cause if I don't I can't go to the movies and all the other kids are going."
>
> His mother is now satisfied, not that he isn't lying, but that he has learned to lie a little better than he did before. She gives Darryl the money, and as an afterthought, she tells him to return the money if he doesn't need it for the movies. The whole family knows that Darryl won't think of returning the money and that's the way it should be.[16]

Playing it cool is a survival technique *par excellence*. Nevertheless, the matter of socialization is not simply training for the cool world as though that world existed in a social vacuum, for that socialization conflicts with those portions of the ghetto world still maintaining working-class orientations and aspirations. Such a world is focused in the mother and the "stable family."

Looking at the street from "inside" the family, one is more aware of the striving for respectability—and the actual accomplishment of the task with certain families at certain times and places. The problem is that at least two, perhaps many more, value configurations or "cultures" influence the lives of those in the ghetto. Which one is given expression at any one time is a matter of circumstance, and which one is dominant or subordinate is not at all clear unless one is willing to acknowledge observable behavior as the only dimension of factuality.

Nevertheless, the problems posed for the young ghetto Negro male by the "cool world" are great, because "being cool" may be an asset in surviving in the street, but it is not a source of deep pleasure. It is rather a source of a great amount of disappointment and sometimes violence, particularly as related to the deception of "cutting out on a spouse." Furthermore, the extent to which a man submerges himself in the cool world is a measure of the acceptance of defeat not only in

[16] Barry Dworkin and Susan Dworkin, "Cool: Young Adults in the Ghetto" (Columbia, Mo.: University of Missouri), p. 4.

the interpersonal realm, but also in the social realm where mobility is still an aspiration. The cool man is not, however, the bowery man who needs assurance from his compatriots that "Man you can't do no better." The cool man has pretentious aspirations in both areas, and the matter of moving up either legitimately or illegitimately is very much a matter of his concern. The need for intimate, affectionate relationships with the opposite sex, while undoubtedly inhibited by the rubric of "cool," nevertheless is there and seeks expression in warm human relationships.

Some of these relationships are quite durable. The family, with all of its internal stresses and strains, exists in spite of the street, though it can never be cut off from it. That it exists with any stability at all in the light of such circumstances is a point that has caused more than one researcher to pause. The argot of cool, the image of the pimp, the life of the street are all too obvious and are on the lips and in the souls of the ghetto dwellers constantly, and yet the solidarity of the family is not completely destroyed.

Portrait of a Ghetto Male at Maturity: Andrew Buchanan

The various themes that have been developed above can be seen reflected in the biographical sketch of a single individual which follows. Here, however, they intertwine with the idiosyncracies of a man's life and loose their clarity as generalizations. Andrew Buchanan, like most older men of the project, was born in the South. He moved to the city when he was twenty. At fifty-five his character has lost much of the rural southern tones, but he has not forgotten what it was like to live there. His experiences are told and retold to his children, particularly to his sons, so that they will understand why their father is as he is.

Recollections of Parents and Childhood

Andrew's father died when he was nine. His father, a "jack of all trades," entered into white culture more than the average Negro male of his town. He managed to keep money in his pocket, food in the pantry, and clothes on his children by keeping "Mr. Charlie" happy. Andrew did not see much of his father because such a job demanded that he be away a lot when "the man" wanted to go hunting or to take a boating excursion on the river.

It was his mother who reared him. He remembers his mother:

> Mother was quite a person, hard working, very critical and resolute in her opinions, almost fanatically religious. . . . I think she was very attractive. She talks, smiles, she was mild of speech; in fact, she was a mild person. She was all woman. . . . *Naturally, I was closer to my mother.* My father was hardly home and my mother was, so I could say in a way I hardly knew my father. . . . My mother was a very critical type of person. She supported what she thought and she done this in every way, so when I didn't do some of the chores, she chastised me physically, and these things came to be unbearable.

This physical chastisement was quite severe:

> To my mother this was to take off all your clothes. She would blindfold you, put something in your mouth, a rag, tie your hands behind you. My mother weighed 215, and she would put you up on a feather bed [150 pound feather mattress] and she set up . . . between your shoulder blades and she got black elm switches—roasted off the bark and tie them together with a wet rag—and what happened between your backbone and your knee joints, you looked like an old washboard.

His mother was the source of all righteousness. She knew what was right and what was wrong. This she implanted in him around the stove on a winter's evening and enforced with elm switches in the bedroom. As a man, he still can say:

> I don't think my life has changed yet, spiritually, I might add. I still think the way my mother and I sat behind the stove and talked, and I'm trying my best to get some of these things accomplished. So my way of thinking hasn't changed. . . . I still like those songs although I don't remember them any more. The things she would like to have me to do when I became a man with a family, children, if I ever had any, that I haven't done. That's

> some of the things I've grieved about. Simple little things that makes me feel my life hasn't changed because I still think the same way I did when I was nine years old sleeping at home with my mother. . . . I see no reason to change, because all the things I thought then I think they are good today. Only they could be better carried out today. I'm not just qualified today as I was then. Maybe educationally I am, but physically I'm not. So I am at a disadvantage.

Sex and Survival

When he ran away from his mother and her unbending justice, he stayed mostly with kin, but sometimes for many months he would be entirely on his own. Wandering from levee camp to "good road camp" to lumber camp, he sharpened his mother wit on the whetstone of grinding poverty. In his teens he learned how to live off the women who kept house in the midst of these work camps. The following is an account of an experience in a lumber camp:

> The lumber company makes these little compounds, and the laborers would in turn get their families a lot of these two or three room houses. [I] don't know how many, but I guess it was a good three to five block area. You go along, single men, single women, families, all kinds of people live here. Some people live there that don't work there at all. So you get in a place like this, get you something to eat, get your clothes washed and take a bath, look for a woman then. You try to find a single one and usually you have a pretty good chance, because you feel like you going to get a job in a day or two. She'll have somebody to give her some money. And they take you in, talk pretty nice, they'll clean you up, give you some of the last old man's clothes, and let you sleep with 'em. *They won't get you a job though.* This time I didn't get a job. I got food, got cleaned up, slept well, got the fifty cents in my pocket and caught the next train.

At another such camp he met a woman that he couldn't pass up too quickly and so he stayed a year with her:

> . . . she was one of the baddest women in the compound; killed two or three people, cut up some men, been at the penitentiary

and all that kind of stuff. She was a desperado to me. I didn't know all this. At the time she was just another woman to me. There was a man who felt the same way she felt. . . . This woman gambled, [was a] commercial prostitute—course she was very attractive—she was young. I guess no more than thirty. I imagine a lot of the men who had wives was always looking at her. This one particular fellow, he was a great big six-footer—looked like an Indian or something—he had long hair, *real light fellow*. We had supper one evening. I was sitting down making me some cigarettes, and she and I was talking. The big guy came in, and he looked at me and said: "Where you come from?" I told him: "I come from Glennon"—that was the last town that I stopped at. "You live down there?" I said: "Yeah." He said: "Why you going up here?" "I'm going to Monroe. . . . I didn't want to live up way in Arkansas." So he said: "You know this is my woman?" "No." "You staying with her?" I said: "Yeah." "You love her?" I said: "Oh yeah, I love her." I'd never say I didn't love a woman. So he say: "You going to stay with her?" I say: "As long as I can." "Well you can't stay here no longer. You got to go right now." I looked at her to see what she was going to say and I guess she made up her mind. She made it up in my favor and she jumped up and say: "No he ain't going nowhere. You going to have to kill us both." Well I guess she know him and I didn't. This scared me to death. *I would fight, but he'd have to have me hemmed up before I would fight*. He told her: "I don't want to have no trouble with you, but you know how I feel about you and I been giving you my money and all this other stuff." She said: "You gave me the money, you can give me some more if you want, but I told you I didn't want you. I tell you get out of here and don't come back any more. . . . As long as this boy wants to stay here he can stay here." So I stayed and he went on out.

So he lived as he traveled around the country, finding a living where he could and always there were women to help. He came to the city in 1930. Times were hard and he continued to rely on his wits and his personality to earn a living city style:

I done what the rest of the guys done. I forgot about going to school. For a time I forgot about traveling, and I got buried down in these hootch joints. Got involved with a lot of women. Had two or three rooms, but couldn't carry no women to my house. In fact, I never really was a lady's man. Having my kind of background, I didn't agree with that sort of thing.

Q: How come?

I found *out early that you had to pay more than you could get to deal with these ladies. They was quite demanding sexually, they slaughter you, and didn't none love you.* At that time (and I still do) I emphasized love. *A woman that I didn't love, I didn't want.*

An auto accident in 1935 "ended this career" and put Andrew in and out of the hospital for about seven years, mainly because he would not stay until sufficiently cured. "I kept coming out; well I was still young and all them bright lights out there, and the situation I was in when I left, why good grief, it was kind of hard to leave."

After getting out of the hospital in 1941 he "fooled around" at various jobs. Finding one at a chicken farm to his liking, he decided to try and extend his work week from just the weekends to a full work week. The man who owned the farm had some notion that "what this nigger needed was a woman more than a salary," and so he offered to board Andrew, pay him his weekend wage for a full week's work, and provide him with a woman:

He brought her up for me, but I knew she was a prostitute so I walked off and left my clothes and everything and that was the end of that job. I went back to the same old rut. I lived all right until I met Betty Re [his wife] in 1944. Then she had irons in the fire. So she and I went up North . . . 'til some time in 1947. I had a good job up there wiping presses. I couldn't get a job when I got back. . . . At this time I didn't have any money so I had nothing to work with. *I was looking to Betty Re having a big time with the boys every night.* I decided this wasn't the way. I got broke, so I knew it wasn't the way. I got to do something. Got a family. I got to live. Although I wasn't married, I had Tracy and Gerald.

There was no concern to marry to prevent an illegitimate birth. Betty Re already had two "outside kids." Nevertheless, there was a concern for the welfare of a "family," and the beginning of a feeling of shame that "this ain't no way to live." Andrew was thirty-three, Betty Re twenty-four when they got married:

> I had no intention of marrying.
>
> *Q:* How did you get hooked?
>
> Well, it was one of those things. I didn't expect to associate myself with a girl who I thought would want children. And I think I was right in that. And so we both were wrong, my wife and me, because we do have the children. But even at that time I had said to myself: "If I had a boy and a girl I would be tickled to death." And that's about all I expected was a boy and a girl. Now these other kids I have [a total of thirteen]. . . . God bless us all.

Race and Place Down Home and in the Promised Land

As a result of being born and raised in Arkansas, he was taught his place. A small matter is remembered:

> Down there we didn't smoke Prince Albert too much because we had to call it *Mr.* Prince Albert. [You had to say this at] any store you went to get it at. Sometimes a white boy'd give us a can after he made his cigarettes. But we didn't ask for it. We didn't like to say "Mr. Prince Albert," so we didn't buy it.

He is quite concerned to point out that the group he ran with in Arkansas did not call each other "nigger" or use the term "Negro," but rather called each other by nicknames.[17]

An incident that "scared him half to death" occurred during one of his several wanderings. He was in a small town in Arkansas:

> I come to a little grocery store, and I saw a lady behind a counter putting some stock on the shelf. She ducked down behind the counter when I walked in. A man was in a little room up near the front door. . . . I come in but hadn't seen him yet, had my back to him. He was shaving and I stood there and knocked on the counter. He didn't stop shaving and the lady didn't come up

[17] "Nigger" is used quite frequently in the project both as a term of camaraderie and degradation. See also its exaltation in Robert H. deCoy, *op. cit.*

from behind the counter. I knew she was there, so I started back out of the door and at the side of it two cases of soda were sitting there. So I picked up one soda bottle—something to quench my mouth—but then I didn't want it. I just threw the soda bottle in the yard next to the store and kept walking. Next thing I know a man run down and caught me. He had about a thirty automatic in his hand. Said, "Give me my soda." I said, "Boss, I don't have it," and he said, "But you got it." "Yes, I got it." He said, "What did you do with it? Drink it up?" And I carried him back. It was still lying in the yard. He said, "Why did you do that?" I said, "I stole it and after I stole it, I didn't want it. I stole it because I'm hungry and I thought a soda would help." "You hungry?" "Yes I am."

There were some ladies, some boys and men [around]—one with a rifle under his arm—he was fixing to shoot a cow. He saw the man with the gun in his hand talking to me so they all surrounded us. Then I got scared.

He said, "You hungry?" "Yes I'm hungry." But then I was hot and scared. I didn't want nothing but to get out of sight. So he said, "Come on." I followed him back up to the store. He got a stool. Gave me the stool. Set me down—the same counter where I had been knocking to get the lady out from behind the counter. That man he cut me bolony, cheese, give me bread and crackers, two or three bottles of cold soda. Never been a big eater. I couldn't eat all that food. He told me, "You wasn't hungry. You lied to me," and I knowed better than to say, "Yes, I was." I just told him, "Mister I eat all I could eat." He said, "You can't no more?" I said, "No sir," and he said, "Oh yes you can! You sit down and eat." I sit down and eat until I puked. That's what I done. When I done that he decided I had enough and he told me to get out of town.

So I went on up to the railroad tracks. I guess I was going north—back towards Arkansas. . . . Right on the middle of the tracks I sat down . . . I sat down and drank some water. I sat there . . . with my sack. Couldn't eat till the train come. . . . You don't have to worry about trains. They don't want you in the town. They don't arrest you about getting *on* trains.

While southern racism is quite straightforward, northern bigotry has its own style. Isolated from respectable people by ghetto living in the North, Andrew's confrontation with "the man" comes more often than not through a policeman. He has encountered the police on many occasions. The following is an account of an attempt to cash a check at a local store. He was authorized to cash checks on a local committee account in order to purchase various items for the community. But he had a problem:

> . . . While writing the check I had made a mistake and put another name on the check. I wanted to erase this off and put the [name of the store] on it and of course this couldn't be permissible because he [the cashier] said the bank wouldn't accept it and I had to get another check. I said well I've got a whole book of checks, but I can't get another check with this man's [the secretary's] name on it and I wanted to know if he wouldn't use this check. While I'm here . . . the police just happened to be in the place while I was talking . . . just browsing. [A policeman came over and said,] "Is this your check?" I said, "Yes." I pointed to the two names on the check and said, "This one is mine, I'm Andrew Buchanan". . . and I went into my pocket to get the statement because I carried this for identification. I carried the letter from the Housing Authority as well.

The police officer would not look at the letter at the store, but took Andrew down to the station and interrogated him. After some time, when a call to the bank convinced the officer that Andrew was who he said he was, he was released. Since he had no carfare, he had to walk about eighteen blocks home.

His reactions to the incident? "Well, he said all the things I had could have been picked up anywhere. I agree with that. He didn't do anything but question me. He didn't put me in jail. He wasn't rough or anything like that." Such incidents are so much a part of his way of life that when told that it would be unlikely that a policeman would intervene in a middle-class person's life in that way, he at first could not believe it. Then he said: "Well, you don't look like a crook and I do—I'm black."

Since he came to the city he has been arrested thirty-three times on charges ranging from "larceny" to "carrying a concealed weapon." His most common charges are "gambling" and "disturbing the peace." He was *convicted only once*. It is difficult to tell from the record if this is the result of police leniency or harassment. Andrew doesn't complain because it is all part of what it means to be black.

On the Job

Andrew has worked at a large variety of jobs for short periods of time. The fact that he has only three years of formal education has always been a handicap which he has partially overcome by using his wits. As a youth, he worked in lumber camps, on "good road" crews, on the levees, and at many other odd jobs. For nearly a year he was a plantation overseer at $50.00 per month. He also learned how to hustle a buck and give an enticing spiel at a carnival. He considers himself a good gambler and loves to play a little policy.

As a young man in the city his legitimate occupations included: paper hanger (which he learned from his mother's brother), cook, gardener, printing press cleaner, laborer on a chicken farm, and while in the hospital for tuberculosis, he learned how to operate power equipment in the "OT" shop, becoming, in effect, a cabinet maker. He sold his products from his shop. His *illegal* occupations include gambling and several years as a pimp for eight or nine prostitutes. Since these do not add up to the total number of years that he has lived in the city, there must be other jobs that he has forgotten to mention as well. His son claimed that he was working for a local manufacturer when he became disabled, but Andrew has not confirmed this. A chronology of his recent employment is as follows:

1932–35—Pimp—also worked a few months as cook in 1933.

1934–41—T.B. hospital which shortly ended his career as a pimp. (For a while he did a bit on the side when out on leave.)

1941—Janitor for a stationery store at 50¢ an hour.

1942—Laborer on a chicken farm, $10.00–$12.00 a day over weekends. Weekday occupation unknown, if any.

1944–47—Press cleaner (lived with Betty Re though unmarried).

1947—Summer bought truck and became a gardener until he broke down from overwork in the fall.

He has not worked full time since 1947. Now on disability because of a pulmonary heart condition, his wife supplements the family's welfare checks with part-time employment. Andrew compensates her by cooking and keeping house, assisted in these tasks by his children.

A Multifaceted Personality

Andrew's physical disability is balanced by an overall dapper appearance. He is now a middle-aged, middle weight man with rather weathered facial features and a smooth personality. He is interesting to talk to because he is interested in almost everything. He wants to "put his best foot forward" and talks on most subjects with a considerable degree of superiority over his peers in the project. In the summer he dresses in a white shirt often without a tie, dark slacks held up by multicolored suspenders, black shoes, and, when going out, a dark brown straw hat.

There are at least four distinct facets to his personality. First, there is the *operator*. The early experience of running away from home has given him a basic cunning which was sharpened by working for a carnival. He describes how he hustled a buck there:

> When you work, you take. You works [for] some guy and he's going to give you a dollar a day. You work all week. Maybe you do get a meal, but you never catch him to get the dollar. You get out of money. Maybe you don't have no way of getting your meals. So you get a guy and say, "Will you see if you can get me somebody . . . to play with me this game and I'll give you ten per cent of whatever they lose?" Well you get into that buck thing and you go out and call some guy in. [You say,] "This guy he always loses, you can win a good prize over here." You talk people in and the more *power*[18] your conversation is the more apt you are to get somebody to play with you. So this is how I got started into this way of talking.

Andrew considers himself to have been a very good gambler at one time and he worked both sides of this gambit. The several arrests on his record suggest a continuing interest.

[18] The word "power" is used often in the project in regard to conversation. Words are recognized as being able to accomplish their intended task, particularly in lovemaking and in putting someone in a trick.

His ability to live off his wits and his power of conversation were very important aspects of his way of life until his health failed and he married. Now he is quite dependent. This component of his personality, consequently, gives a rather rich overtone to his pattern of speech and a certain style and polish to his mannerism—for example, he prefers English oval cigarettes when he can buy them.

The dominant public image that he puts forth is bifocal. On the one hand he is *the concerned citizen:*

> I'm highly interested and I feel that if I gather some of the information that they [government officials] be putting out so freely here that I might be able to advance myself or help somebody advance who is more qualified than me and who doesn't have the time to go get out and gather the information. . . . I feel that these things would be helpful to me and to my family and for my community by making me what you might say, a better citizen.

He also feels that he might be of some use as an informant on the problems of poverty and says, "I'm just full of ideas but I don't know how good they are. . . . [Nevertheless,] I appreciate talking for public use."

On the other hand, he feels incompetent and has strong tendencies toward *melancholia.* "I'm not qualified, at least I don't feel qualified to motivate anything." He traces his melancholy mood to the fact that he never really knew his father:

> I loved my father, but I just didn't see him enough, so I became, I guess, melancholy and quite lonely. As a man I am still that way. . . . Pure loneliness was my motivation for leaving home, and of course my mother's strict discipline.

When he was young, he used to cope with this loneliness by traveling to different places and listening to the stories of other men and women, stories that stirred his imagination.

> The fact that you had to strive so hard for survival you forgot it. All your thoughts was of people who made you happy, the conversation, the newness of it sometimes is a revelation to a young boy to hear an old man talk about San Francisco, New York, Niagra Falls. He never dreamed these things existed.

Andrew still has an "itch in his heel," but he no longer travels the rails to relieve it. More and more nowadays, he is overcome with depression and withdraws within himself or goes out for a night on the town. Drinking occupies more of his time now, and he doesn't seem to understand why it does.

A fourth and quite basic part of his self-image is the way in which he sees himself *as a Negro*. This image is informed by intimate and degrading experiences both in the South and in the North, and tempered by a much better than average acquaintance with the literature on the Negro. Among the books that he has read on the subject are: *The Myth of the Negro Past, Dark Ghetto, The Negro Family: The Case for National Action,* and numerous short stories of the Negro in America. All of these were personally selected, and in the case of the *Negro Family,* at least, he manifests considerable comprehension, an amazing accomplishment in light of his very poor formal education.

There are many events that have left their imprint on his memory and thereby shape his conception of what it is to be a Negro. Like every other Negro coming out of the South, he has had it impressed upon him that "a nigger ain't nobody." The North has not gone very far to convince him otherwise. But he is somebody after all. Here, then, is how Andrew talks about "his people." The problems of everyday existence are many and mold a people in strange ways. Negro parents indulged their children a great deal. He says:

> You see, I put it this way. . . . Most of us are loose type of people and therefore we are prone to things. Not *that we designed that way but we are prone to it because we live in such situations that it's always before us.* And of course it's hard to resist any one subject too long without it getting to you.

One subject that gets to you is the problem of having too little money around the house:

> . . . That's why some guys will go out and stick up a filling station or turn to crime and perhaps he has a limited mind. He don't know anything else to do . . . but take something for his family. . . . Therefore when somebody comes along and he see you with ten dollars, he'll snatch it or hit you up side the head or

something of that nature. Then you will say, "Well these colored people down here is awful." Well, you know, one must eat.

His major theme on the subject of race is repeated on every suitable occasion. "I just felt that there was no such people [as the Negro] and why, I don't know. I just felt that without any support for it at all." By this he means that given half a chance, the Negro will live like the white man. There is an American culture in his eyes and differences in skin color are more than compensated for by the similarity in way of life—at least as far as what is considered to be the desirable way of life. This naturally leads him to the point where he thinks that it is silly for social scientists to be interested in the kinds of things the Negro does because the Negro wants the same kind of things that everyone else does. Andrew is thus, in the light of recent black separatism, a "Negro" in the fullest sense.[19]

Once, after reading an article in the *Negro Digest* entitled, "The Value of Black Indignation," he went on to say that the "Buchanan of thirty years ago would stoop and ask the white man, 'Do you have any money please for a hungry man?' and be turned down by *the man*, but the Buchanan of today knows how to act properly."

Since November 1965, he has withdrawn more and more from his attempts at self-improvement and has dropped a large portion of his interest in the community. He sees himself as a failure but, nevertheless, cannot get rid of his great expectations. They make his failure more painful:

> I haven't done any good to my estimation. Some say I have, and I can see a few things. I hear people talk. They talk my talk. And I see some people using my ideas, so I feel in this way I've done a little good. But to me this is not what I would like to achieve, not to achieve what you call greatness, but something that would be outstanding and become institutionalized is what I would like to establish. When I could do something like this then I would think I have done something to my own satisfaction. . . . I

[19] DeCoy, *op. cit.*, p. 33: "Negro, n. adj. A vulgar but accepted description of the Nigrite or Nigger. Referring to an American Nigger of decency and status. A White-Nigger. Or a brainwashed Black who would be Caucasian if possible. A Nigger who desires to be and would believe himself a social factor in the modern American complex."

would like to do this kind of thing for the benefit of the community . . . something that the community can use for years as long as the community exists. They can use particular programs because it's good and lasting. Way down in somebody's heart they would say, "Old man Buchanan done that." I would be proud. This to me is like going to heaven. This to me means you had a good spirit.

His efforts have largely gone unrewarded over the years. Despite all of his ability at provocative talk, he cannot find anybody in the community to "carry the ball" when he cannot. Most of the persons he deals with outside of the family do not understand him or they do not share his interest. He, therefore, describes himself as a "man in between"—a man in between two worlds, the world of the street where the men constantly work game, talk of sports and women, and get high; and the world of the larger society as he experiences it through his contacts in the project and the larger war on poverty.

Familial Status and Phantom Role

Andrew has been married over seventeen years. The majority of this time he has not been the major source of the family's income. His case suggests a further modification of the Parsonian position on family status which asserts essentially that a man's status in the family is mainly dependent upon his status in the community. This is because he performs the instrumental role where he is the link between the family and the community at large.[20] Mr. Buchanan complains of low status within his family. Specifically, he complains that his wife manages the budget and his children respect her more than they do him. At first glance it would seem that this would be consistent with Parsonian views on the matter, since Andrew is not employed and his disability check is less than his wife's ADC check. However, in point of fact, he has a great deal more status within the family than he generally acknowledges. His children quite regularly ask him for permission to go out or to do various things around the house; his wife consults with him on her decision to take or not to take

[20] Talcott Parsons and Robert Bales, *Family Socialization and Interaction Process* (New York: The Free Press, 1955), p. 13.

various jobs that are offered to her. She does not openly disagree with her husband in front of the children and quite often compliments him on his ideas. What seems to account for the difference between observation and interview on this point is that the husband is evaluating himself on the social status scale of the larger community, which says that a man must work if he is to be considered a man. Because he has always had aspirations of upward mobility along this scale of evaluation, it is more important in his thinking than the evaluation of his wife and children. In their eyes, however, he has managed to achieve more status than a man in his position might ordinarily. In part this is so because he has developed what might be called "a phantom role." [21] This role is not a pretense so much as it is an exaggeration that becomes so real that even the actor sometimes is fooled. It has, in this regard, the elements of a self-fulfilling prophecy. Andrew's phantom role is that of the competent educated man who cannot realize the benefits of an education because of a physical handicap.

This image is maintained by a number of factors: first of all, he has a library containing several dozen books in his bedroom; secondly, he has developed a series of contacts with educated people—social workers, community organizers, social scientists, and clergy, to whom he presents the inside picture of what it is like to be a poor Negro man. He takes adult courses in public speaking, attends conferences, and calls meetings together to discuss the problems of project life. During the day he sometimes is seen composing speeches or reading a book. More often he is sleeping. His children believe that he quite often stays up late at night at his studies—an excuse he uses for the fact that he usually sleeps until noon or thereafter. His children think that he is "the greatest" and often whisper words of praise of their father.

Yet, despite his professed emphasis upon education, he does not stress the fact that his children should be in school, nor help them by seeing that they get to work on their homework. The family directly benefits from his phantom role, however, by being the recipients of a larger amount of welfare and free gifts—new beds, furniture, clothes. It is difficult, therefore, to say that Andrew is a complete phony—he is a very perceptive man who has learned how to work the system

[21] This term was coined by the research staff.

quite efficiently. He has merely projected his image along more acceptable lines, and the phantom nature of the role that he plays can be seen only when we view his behavior against more widely accepted expectations associated with the role.

The Pain of Awareness

Andrew once heard a learned man speak on poverty. He came away with the feeling that he had been listening to things with which he was quite familiar. Big time people were talking about poverty, and he was intimately acquainted with the problem of poverty as it impinged on the American Negro. Two things came out of this: first, he was pleased to find that his information was not out of date; and second, he became aware of the fact that many people were making money off the poor. He once told the author that he felt he was a person "who was trying to get something for nothing." He is aware of the fact that there are people who, because of their contact with the poor, make quite nice salaries. This disturbs him.

When another member of the research team once came to the family to talk about Clinton's school problems, he asked her quite straightforwardly: "I can see what you can get from being with Clinton and Annette, but what would they get from you?" He hopes it will be a solution to their problems. "If you find out what's wrong with him, we'd certainly appreciate it if you would let us know."

So many persons have studied the families in the project, however, that he has developed a certain basic disgust at the questions often asked. He expressed it this way:

> It's like they used to do in the old days, they say, "Colored people keep coming out here asking about pork chops and we gone form a committee to see why they like pork chops." You know, its everyday. You can say, "Heck, I get tired of eating beans and greens and things, I'd like to have a steak." And I mean everything—they have to go into a great deal of research and things and when you want the things the other man want. . . . It's a waste of everybody's time 'cause people seem to know and they just give you a bunch of lies.

He has had his share of researchers. His black indignation has not been completely buried beneath his "Negro" front.

Conclusions

The data suggest the following generalizations:

1. The conception of what it means to be a man includes an image of a father who was a hard working field hand or unskilled laborer "almost essential" to his employer—a man under such constraints that he must accommodate himself to "the man's" wishes and "walk around him."

2. In the city, boys help out around the house, but the traditional chores of country life are no longer needed. The girl's chores remain largely the same. The father is, furthermore, less able to provide an effective role model for his son than the mother is for her daughter.

3. Boys are more influenced by their peers than girls in the sense that much more of their early socialization centers around the gang than around the home. The gang furthers the process of breaking away from the mother begun in playing the dozens, and the father has more of an impact upon his son's "coming up" after this process is completed.

4. The strategy of "cool" creates tensions for ghetto males because, while it enables one to effectively control the situation, it also makes it more difficult to achieve intimate relationships. A mother may thus teach her son how to be cool with some ambivalence, for it is an aid to survival in the street, but tends to be a barrier to domestic intimacy.

5. Familial status in families is sometimes attained by the maintenance of a "phantom role" enabling the actor to live not so much a lie as a fervent desire to be something more than he is. Such a role is partially supported by most members of the family most of the time. It's hollowness can be seen best by comparison to the expectations associated with the role in the larger society.

Chapter 4

Conflict and the Quest for Intimacy

Masculine and feminine roles take on new dimensions when a family is formed. In the middle-class perception of what is appropriate, one first becomes a husband or a wife and then assumes the role of a father or mother. While this ideal is not completely realized in middle-class life, in the ghetto the sequence is more often reversed. Indeed, it would seem one typically assumes the parent role before the spouse role. In this small group of parents only one mother, Leona Wards, neither had a child nor conceived one before marriage. In six of the ten instances a marriage could be said to have been "triggered" by pregnancy.

In part this is so because sex is perceived as natural and parents do not as a rule forbid "doing it" as long as pregnancy does not result. At least to some extent this results from the agonistic character of sex role development which pits the sexes against each other in a zero sum contest that is a constant feature of ghetto life. These aspects of the problem of marriage have already been discussed. Other equally if not more important factors that make lifelong monogamous marriage difficult in the ghetto will be discussed in the next chapter. Here it is appropriate to focus upon the quality of the marital relationship itself and the alternative relationships that develop as adaptations to the harsh deprivations of ghetto existence.

Even in such a small number of families as ten, the experience of the complete families is quite different than that of the incomplete, but this does not justify viewing the lower-class Negro family as simply either complete or incomplete. Rather, the data suggest a much wider variety of types that can be described and analyzed largely by focusing upon the extent to which the adult male participates in the life of and contributes to the support of his woman and her family. A seven-fold typology of male marginality is suggested.

THE FIVE COMPLETE FAMILIES

The Billits

The Billits have been married about seven years. He is forty-four and she is thirty-one. It is his second marriage; his first ended after nine years, when he discovered that his wife was "cutting out" with a fifty-two-year-old man who wasn't even earning as much as he. The Billits have between them a total of four children born outside, including Margie who was born to them before marriage and Camella who is not Stanley's child. The other outsiders live with their mother.

Stanley Billit claims he left his first wife in style:

> I sent her to the grocery store. When she come back from the grocery store with the groceries I had done laid all my clothes out on the bed. She said, "What are you fixing to do?" I said, "I'm fixing to let you go," so she started to cry.

However, after he left her he "went crazy":

> I stayed with so many women, I don't know how many it was. . . . If they didn't act right I'd leave them and get somebody else. . . . For two years everytime I looked at a woman I hated the ground they walked on. I thought they was all just alike.

He claims he spent some $2,000 in savings "living it up" while out of wife and job.

Alliena, his wife, is proud of the fact that her mother is a "very attractive woman and still has men friends." Her mother and father fought and for the better part of her marriage her mother gave in—but when she finally stood up to him she never gave in again. Alliena is adamant:

> Now my daddy whipped my mama and beat and scrawled and run her out barefooted [in the winter time] but it ain't a man alive today that I think I'm going to just stand up and let him do

> that to me. . . . I vowed that I wouldn't let a meatman hit and beat on me.

The Billits met in 1956. She was living next door to his sister, although it was some time before Alliena discovered that the woman whom she admired so much was the sister of her husband. By the time she did he had already moved in with her and her roommate. They lived together common law for "four or five years" before they finally got married. Stanley says, "I would have married her long before she wanted to marry but it took a long time for her to make her mind up." Alliena replied, "And I didn't make it up then." Their marriage was, according to Alliena:

> . . . a spur of the moment thing. My mother had come over one Saturday to visit and spent the night and she told me, "Oh, you're just disgracing me." . . . I wasn't pregnant then because the baby was born. She told me, "I wish you would done get married."
>
> *Stanley:* She was telling you right.
>
> *Alliena:* Yeah, she was telling me right, but as I look at it now she was living with a man and she's going to tell me I'm disgracing her.
>
> *Stanley:* Aw, he just stayed with her a couple of nights.
>
> *Alliena:* A couple of nights my eye. He bought her the rings and everything, but she hadn't got a divorce from daddy. . . . I guess I took two hundred blood tests. I'd change my mind and come back home, but this time we went on down there and got this blood test and went on and got married.

Why marry? Stanley says, "Because I loved her!" but then he expresses his more calculated motives:

> I'd rather be married than just staying with a woman. . . . I figure that if you're just staying with a woman and you're not married to her, she's as much somebody else's as she is yours. . . . And if you jump on the man [for taking her out] the first thing he'll say is "Well, she ain't none of yours. . . . You ain't got no papers on her." Where . . . if that's your wife, can't nobody say nothing. . . . If [you] want to whip her [you] can whip her.

The Billits constantly bicker and quarrel, but they have fought only twice. Once was over Stanley's walking around in front of his daughters "in an ornery sort of way." The neighbors complain that he handles their young daughters, and this is probably the basis of Alliena's concern. His nudity as such does not bother her. The second fight took place over Alliena's claim that Stanley had taken her ADC check and spent part of it on another woman. He hit her over the eye with an ash tray that time and now warns, "Well, if I didn't love you, I would have killed you. . . . [aside] She's the only woman I had I didn't beat. I'd whip them. All my women was scared of me."

The Billits were once asked about the bad things in their marriage. They replied in what developed into an argument:

> *Stanley:* I don't think it's no bad things. It's whatever you make. . . . That woman there, she's so mean I don't know what to say. She cuss and go on and call me all kinds of names. . . . Sometimes I come in and say, "You got dinner done?" "Naw, I ain't got dinner done. *You* cook!" She think I should get up and cook my own dinner or breakfast. I don't figure like that.
>
> *Alliena:* . . . That man never walks in that door with a smile on his face. Never! He keeps his face all screwed up. He never walks in that door with a smile on his face. I'm ready to throw everything including the kitchen sink at him. . . . Moreover he thinks I know everything and that I think he doesn't know anything. . . . But he says, "I'm the man of the house and what I say goes—right or wrong." And I just can't go along with that. . . . He says, "Live today and forget about tomorrow," but I can't do that because I have children and I see their tomorrow, not so much as my own . . . [and] it's just little things. Like putting linoleum on the floor. I'll ask him a whole year. I'll say, "*My* floor needs a linoleum on it. Will you get me one?" He'll walk around, well, hell, he don't give a "who shot John" about the house. When I go get it, it's an argument. . . .
>
> *Stanley:* Aw, that woman, she's I don't know what to say. I don't like for no woman to get nothing unless she tells me about it. I don't care what it is what she do is, a lot of times she go and get things and I don't know what she done got until she done brought it here. . . .

Alliena has a year of college and Stanley has only one year of school. His ability to function has been further impaired by an injury suffered in a fight about three years ago that entitled him to disability. Stanley continues the attempt to establish himself as the effective head of the household. He expects to play the husband-father role as commonly conceived by the middle class, with perhaps even a slightly patriarchal emphasis in spite of everything. The house, however, is *her* house. "*My* floor needs linoleum." The car is his. Their money is separate due to the fact that they both receive government checks, which they conveniently think of as "his money" and "her money."

Their squabbles over money matters likewise stress small things. He is angry because she doesn't charge everyone for using her washing machine. She claims that she does and laments, "If I had the money he's spent on cars in the last two months, which is approximately $80.00, I could have a whole new living room of furniture."

A final contrast is that he goes to church regularly and she doesn't (a reversal of the norm for churchgoers in the project). He complains, "That woman cuss so much, I don't know why she don't go to church. Maybe she could change her ways." Alliena, on the other hand says, "I cannot go to church and come back Sunday morning calling names." As a matter of fact she attempted once to make up this deficit by going on Wednesday evening to prayer meeting, but he suspected her of "cutting out." She complains:

> . . . I trust him. He can go where he wants to go and do what he wants to do. . . . If he enjoys going out with women, sure he can go out with other women. Because you see, I don't want to kill him. I tell him all the time. I don't want to be his death for nothing. And if he don't find enjoyment here with me and he can find it out in the street, then go out in the street.

To this he retorted, "Aw, the other night when I went back to the hospital with a boy, I didn't come back until five o'clock and she swore I was with some other woman. I was sitting up at the hospital with him." Alliena countered:

> All these things you see I've had reason to believe. I'd be having my belly sticking way out here and vomiting every fifteen minutes and he'll walk out of here and leave me and go over to [the East

> side] and when he dresses up I know that he going over there to good time and party . . . but when he gets in jail, I'm the one he calls on for the $200.00 bond money.

The suspicion of both spouses is evident. One of the most characteristic features of all male/female relationships is extreme jealousy and the demand that affection be constantly demonstrated. The Billits' problem is heightened by their totally different interests and divergent educations. Alliena sees her present position in life as a terrible setback from her ambitions to become a school teacher.

Their bickering is carried over into every aspect of their married life. Sexually, Stanley is able to dominate his wife. He is able to get her to bed frequently, satisfy himself, and leave her "hung up in the air." She complains, "Out of four times since Sunday [recorded on a Friday], I've been satisfied once." Frustration seems to be a way of life for Alliena. Her response is generally straightforward aggression against her husband. He, for his part, seems only too willing to spar. Being nothing of a match for her sharp tongue, he is usually beaten in such verbal duels. He then goes out and "good times and parties."

Stanley has problems with his children as well. Louise, his last and only legitimate child, caught pneumonia when she was one year old, and some complications arising out of that illness have retarded her development and left her at the age of six unable—or unwilling—to speak. She is a very unruly and demanding child. He tries to meet as many of her demands as he can when he is in the house. Most of the responsibility, however, is placed in the hands of Camella, his nine-year-old stepdaughter. He is angered by the fact that she is prettier and smarter than either of his two girls. All of the children, but particularly Camella, the oldest, address their requests to their mother rather than their father when they enter the room.

Alliena never wanted any of her children. All of them came with great pain and difficulty after long illnesses. Once she thought she was pregnant and remarked, "I need another baby like a hole in the head. . . . But of course he thinks it's great." As a mother she is not overly demonstrative of affection, does not give a great deal of evidence of concern for her children's activities outside the home (such as their schooling), and delegates whatever work she can within the household to her daughters. It would be too harsh to say that she merely tolerates her children; rather, it seems that she is too much caught up in her own problems to be very deeply concerned about them.

Since her husband is not working, Alliena refuses to "fix for" him and he either fixes for himself or has Cam do it. Camella and Margie ordinarily ask permission of their mother to do various things without consulting their father. Louise works on the emotions of all the members of the household and ordinarily gets her way without the necessity of speaking. She manages her father much more easily than her mother.

Stanley's attitude toward his own children is an interesting mixture of affection and disappointment. He tends to handle them tenderly but rather ineptly. When their mother is present, he has little control over their activities. Thus he is quite marginal to his household. He is bound to his wife in strong but ambivalent ways, summed up in his warning, "If I didn't love you, I would have killed you," which seems to reflect his intense concern to become the "head of the house." He cannot do this with Alliena in the way he claims he used to with his other women —that is, by beating her. He is not able to demand her obedience because he is not able to do much for her (either economically or sexually). His wife is to a great extent a matter of sexual property, and marriage is the best way he sees of protecting it. With such a conception of marriage, his affection is focused on his children.

Stanley's self-esteem depends heavily upon a conception of himself as a hardworking, industrious man. The first impression he wanted to make in recounting his life was the fact that he "began to plow at eight" and how he thinks of himself as earning $150.00 a week even though he is unemployed because this is the wage earned by members of his old construction crew. His car comes before his home, and his caring for his children is more a matter of small things, such as helping Louise on with her shoes, than it is a matter of sacrificing for their welfare.

The Billits are constantly quarreling, in part because they do not have a complementary conception of their roles as parents and spouses. One wonders that such a marriage can long endure, but it has lasted over seven years, and although there is constant bickering, it may well last a number of years longer. Despite his wife's harping, he is relatively happy with the arrangement, and Alliena, despite her disappointment with her marriage, fears men and dislikes the street life too much to seek out another man. At least she has managed, for the most part, to prevent this one from beating her. It is far from the best of all possible worlds, but it minimally meets the needs of all its members at present.

The Pattersons

Although the Pattersons have been married for twenty-two years, their marriage has been broken on several occasions by his desertion, at least three times before the family moved to the city and two or more times since. Each time he has come back. Each time she has accepted his promise to try to "do right," and each time he has disappointed her. At present the family is together, but the internal rumblings indicate that another rupture is near at hand.

Between them the Pattersons have eight "outsiders," all but two being his and none now living with them. At present their household includes eight legitimate children, from nine to nineteen in age. Mr. Patterson is the major source of the family's income, his wages contributing $466 to the family's $506 monthly income. His wife's earnings make up the rest, giving the family an annual income of $6,072.

Edward Patterson has an obvious split in allegiance. Several women and their children vie for his affection and support.[1] He allowances his wife and expects her to live within that allowance, adequate or not, while his spending extends to his several outside children. Some of these children live in the city with a woman he has kept for a number of years. His wife has been fully and painfully aware of this. About four years ago he left his family to live with this woman for two years. During this time his wife was on ADC. Prior to that, in 1955, she put him in the workhouse for six months for nonsupport.

Edward is a dark brown, trim, but very muscular man standing about six feet tall with the large hands of a farmer and the quick wit and ready smile of a man used to the city. His manners are above reproach, and the impression he gives is always that of a gentleman—controlled congeniality. However, because of the way he has treated his family in the past he has lost their respect. Indeed, he has courted their scorn. As a result he eats alone almost every evening. Della Mae will "fix for him" and talk with him occasionally, but normally he is

[1] His arrangement with the women in his life recalls that of Papa Sanchez. Oscar Lewis, *The Children of Sanchez* (New York: Random House, Inc., 1961).

left to himself. He, therefore, has rather guarded comments to make about his marriage:

> I would say that if I had to do it over again I don't think I would select this route that I have gone. It hasn't been too pleasant at all times . . . [because of a] lack of understanding between the two of us. . . . I mean there's a ruling to everything. You can't run in the house and what's on the outside of the house both at the same time. . . . So I don't know whether I just stayed on the outside too long. It's a problem somewhere. . . . I don't think it would get serious enough where it would cause another separation. . . . [You] make the best out of what you have. . . . I take whatever it is and go along with it as long as it's nothing hurting me. . . . I can walk, shun them, a lot easier than the other person could shun me.

His wife's account of their marriage is more direct:

> Well before we came to [the city] my husband and I were separated three times on the sake of fighting. He used to fight me all the time. He was in the city about nine months before I came. When I came up he was living with another woman at my uncle's house. . . . I have never walked out in front of him. But this lady he used to live with, he have had her right out in front of my door. . . . The first time he brought her down there I didn't say anything so I asked him not to do it again, because he seemed like he was boasting about it. And the next time he did it . . . I got a gun and started down the steps and he ran down there by the car. But by the time I got down under the building he had done pulled off.

Edward came back from living with this woman about two years ago and promised to do better. Della Mae says, "I felt that these was his kids and rather than to marry some other man I'll guess I just as soon go ahead on and put up with him if he wants to do right. . . . He did for about two months . . . so now I don't feel I could ever let him come back again." According to her he does not want to leave because it will cost him too much in child support.[2]

[2] One of the problems encountered in family studies is the fact that it is difficult to maintain equally good relations with all members of the family. In this

Edward does not get along well with his children, particularly his older boy Andrew, who has moved out to live with a sister in order to avoid a fight with his father, who "hit him up side of the head with a shoe." Edward's violence disturbs his wife. "When he walks in the door the actual sight of him makes me nervous . . . because I have a fear of his ways."

Edward feels "overrun by kids" also. He once hurt his daughter Glennora by exclaiming, "There just too many children in this house." Although she no longer feels close to her father, she, nevertheless, tones down the family feuding:

> . . . Every family has its ups and downs. You know, like sometimes the financial situation is good and they can buy a couple of things for the house and buy everybody in the house something. And then again the financial problems are down. . . . My father, I think he budgets his money and that's a nice thing for a family as large as ours. Therefore I think it's pretty nice. . . . He's okay. Like if he be mad he's not okay . . . *but he will give*. Like if we need something and come to him. If he have it to spare he'll give to us and if he haven't got it to spare he won't. My mother is really nice. I guess all kids feel that way about their mother because the mother be with them mostly all the time when the father is at work. And when you're sick she's always there. She goes out of her way to do things for us and whatever she can do to help us we can always depend on her. . . . Some parents be arguing and fighting all the time. All parents quarrel sometimes, but they don't hardly quarrel. Like if they be angry at each other they might say a couple of words and let it go at that. One of them will walk away from it. I guess because they have us and *don't want to be setting a bad example in front of us.*

While both parents are described in terms of what they do for their kids, the image of her mother is much more favorable in its emotional overtones. There is a stronger impression of dependability. Most chil-

---

case I met the wife first, so the husband would not bring up his marital problems directly, and as a result her view of the situation predominates, counterbalanced, however, by observation and interviews with other members of the family.

dren will say that their daddy is a good father because he will always "give to them," but Glennora tempers this standard statement with "if he has it to spare" and "if he is not mad." She interprets his control of the money as a good thing, whereas her mother feels that it is tyrannical. Her mother also resents the "outside" distribution. Glennora knows of these indiscretions but she nevertheless presents the best impression. She likewise favorably interprets the fact that the parents do not argue before their children and implies that it is because they have their tempers under control. Another interpretation might suggest that they "walk away" because they are unable to control themselves.

Della Mae gives this account of a family episode that occurred after Andrew left to live with his sister, in order to avoid a fight with his father:

> The next morning when I got up I couldn't eat I was so nervous. I said, "You're making me nervous." He said, "If you're nervous, get out." J. J. [her son] said, "Daddy you ought to be ashamed of yourself. You know mother ain't been long having a hemorrhage and it looks like you're trying to get her upset." He said, "Get your mamie and get out of here." So Glennora said, "Lord have mercy, what kind of a family is this? We're supposed to be a family and everybody's arguing. This ain't no way for a family to do." He said, "It's too damn many in this family." She said, "Lord have mercy, I ain't got nothing else to say." . . . Glennora is a very easy child.

Despite the possible distortions of hearsay evidence, it seems likely that the children did side with Della Mae against Edward. They do this ordinarily. Glennora *is* an easy child, rather retiring and most diligent in her homework. She tries to pretend the family *is* like it *ought* to be.

Madeline, now living outside the household, gives this perspective of her father:

> He was a lot better then [when she was six] than he is now because at that time he used to smile more and everything. Now whatever you say anything to him or not he seems like he's withdrawn into himself. He acts like he's mad at the world. . . . It seems like she [her mother] can't do anything to satisfy him. I

> mean if she fixes dinner he don't want it or either he'll walk in the house and he'll look at it and walk out the door.

Della Mae is considerably shorter than her husband. She is heavy set and rather slow moving. She has a tendency to make the most out of her illnesses. The hemorrhage that J. J. talks about was of a small blood vessel in her nose, which wouldn't stop bleeding for a number of hours. She laid around the house for over three weeks complaining of her hemorrhage when anyone would listen. She sees herself as "a nice person":

> If I know a person is at least half way right, I'll go along with them. I takes more than the average person would no matter what a person does to me. I never argue back. I don't believe in arguments. I never was a spoiled child. I never give my mother and father no kind of trouble. I was a very good child.

Della Mae met Edward at a country store and they were married after a year of courting, in spite of her mother's prophecy, "You can marry him if you want to but he's going to make you cry many days because he's not the man for you. . . . He's not going to treat you like you should be treated by a man and as kind as you is." Yet despite her grievances, she claims that she has never "cut out" on him:

> I just don't believe in it. My mother always talked against such things and I've never been that type. I had had people to tell me that. "Why don't I do that?" I just can't do it. I know I have made up my mind and even dressed to do it, but I'd go back and pull my clothes off and set right here with the kids.

Part of Edward's reluctance to leave is his concern over child support, since she might be able to get more from him if he walks out on her than she is able to at present. Another factor, however, must certainly be his own sexual problems. She once confided that her husband was not able to satisfy himself sexually and that this caused him considerable embarrassment and concern over his virility. Such a concern would, in all probability, contribute to his tendency to stay around home.

Edward is marginal to his family in quite another way than William Billit, who has never spent extended periods of time away from home since marriage. Because he has a good job, the child support that could be extracted if he left his family is something that puts pressure on him to stay at home. His sexual embarrassment also contributes to this current tendency. He cannot, however, cut his ties with "what's outside." He says, "That's my responsibility and it's my problem." His own house has too many children in it, his wife does not understand him, and, since the marriage has broken down in the past, there is no reason to suppose that it will not continue to do so in the future. And yet he cannot break permanently. His efforts to do what's right by both "what's inside and what's outside" are a source of continual strain to his wife and children. His home life is all but intolerable; yet while he is home he controls the economy with an iron hand. "I makes my money and I can spend it the way I want to."

The Washingtons

Although the Washingtons have been visited for over three-and-one half years, they remain largely unknown. Arthur (fifty-one) and his wife Lotta (forty-seven) have both worked most of the time during the day and are often not at home at night. When visiting them, one is always well received and feels relatively at home, except for an awareness that the conversation is quite controlled. This caution has at least a partial explanation. Arthur has a long record of arrests going back to 1939, connected in the main with gambling but involving only two convictions. The last one sent him to the workhouse for thirty days for being caught with lottery equipment. Seven of his sons also have records of arrests for gambling, and two have convictions and imprisonments for narcotics violations. His wife and daughters, however, do not have any arrests.

He and his wife have been married twenty-six years. Arthur says that he has managed to stay married that long because, "We don't raise a lot of cain. If a little something happens we don't jump down each other's throat." He expresses his conception of marital fidelity in such a way that implies he "cuts out" but does not play the field and does not brag about his antics in front of his wife:

> I am this type of fellow. I talk to anybody before my wife or behind my wife. But just to go out and say I've got a bunch of

> women and that type of thing, that's all baloney. . . . I see some women that look good to me, sure, and if you push it you can get caught in the right corner and you might step out. You're human and you're a good one if you don't. If you just go out and strive directly for that then you're going to find somebody that wants to do those things. The average woman that does it ain't doing it because she likes to but she wants to do something just like you . . . something different . . . it's not a big thing.

His wife presents the complimentary picture of her going along with his discreet outside activities:

> I think I've been a nice lady. I ain't bragging on myself, but it takes a steady head I guess. I never was a wild person and liked to get in the streets. I stayed home and took care of my children. . . . I didn't leave my children with nobody.

Lotta is a southern woman raised on the farm. She was thirteen when she met her first boyfriend, went with him a couple of months, and then met her husband, whom she married when she was about eighteen, after having "gone with him" for about a year. She had known his sister before meeting him. She got married primarily because, "My mother was kind of strict on me. . . . I said if I could get married I would come to the city. I think that's the real reason I got married. I was in a nice home and everything but I had got to the point where I really thought she was too strict." They lived with his mother for about six months, then moved to the city. Two of the first three children born to her died within the first year. Arthur was more experienced with women than his wife was with men before they married. "I was a fast little boy, I didn't have too many girlfriends. I had about three that I could call girlfriends."

They were married at the courthouse with only his mother and the best man attending.

Lotta now says that by and large she is satisfied with her marriage:

> Sometimes I said I wish I hadn't gotten married. Of course I have quite a few children but I think my life has been pretty good. My husband has been very nice. He does the best he can. *We haven't been separated* and we raised our children up as far as we got them. So I don't think we done such a bad job.

The Washington house is in good condition and always has been, despite the fact that eight persons live in it. Arthur explains:

> . . . You just don't allow your kids to tear things up. You just keep the kids from playing on it. [You] just say, "Look you just don't do that. If you do, you're going to get a whipping." Once you tear them real good they ain't going to do it no more. Some people say, "I love my children and nothing I've got is too good for them and it's mine and I paid for it. If they want to play on it let them play on it." [But] I don't see it that way. . . . I don't let them play on my car . . . that's my living. . . . My kids don't play on my furniture. . . . When I work for them and give them a place it ain't too much trouble I'm going to have. You've just got to be a man. . . .

Another impressive indicator of the control these parents have over the children is their willingness not to give gifts at Christmas time. Arthur says, "It's pretty rough when you know everybody else is receiving them and giving them and you're not . . . but if you understand life . . . you just have to grit your teeth and say, well we doing the best we can, and thank the Lord."

Finally, rather than denouncing delinquent children as many parents would, Arthur refused to tell the police of his son Terry's whereabouts, even though this child has given him the most trouble of any of his children and has the longest and most serious record. He says simply, "He's just another one of my kids regardless of the troubles he's been in. Maybe he made a mistake and maybe he didn't. Maybe he just got the wrong break. That happens too. Sometimes to the best of people."

It is apparent that the family, despite what goes on outside, *is* a central concern for Arthur. He is much more a part of its life than either Stanley Billit or Edward Patterson. His discretion in handling what goes on outside is a major factor in contributing to its stability. At one time he was the major wage earner. However, as his family increased in size he supplemented its income with proceeds from the numbers racket and his odd jobs. This deviant career has been well copied by his boys. Unlike both Stanley Billit and Edward Patterson, he manifests interest in the management of his household and children and does some of the work around the house himself to help his wife when she is working. His relationship with his wife is much more than a marriage of convenience, and although "cutting out" is a part of his pattern, he has done it with discretion, and both agree, "We get along well enough." Arthur Washington has thus been able to teach his boys a form of behavior that will give them an edge in survival in the street, but will be a handicap in terms of their movement out of the ghetto because it is perceived as illicit behavior by those outside. At the same time he is concerned about their deviance and would rather credit their records to "bad breaks" than to their being bad boys because he is interested that they "make a go of it" legitimately if at all possible. If not, then you "do the best you can."

The Buchanans

Andrew Buchanan (fifty-five) and his wife Betty Re (forty-seven) have been married eighteen years. This is his first and her second marriage. Together they have raised thirteen children, including two "outsiders." Three of their children are married and they now have thirteen grandchildren, all of whom at one time or another have lived with the Buchanans for an extended period. At present their five-bedroom apartment contains only sixteen persons.

Andrew ran away from home when he was nine, was taken into the homes of relatives until he was in his twenties, and reestablished contact with his mother when he came to the city in the 1930s. Betty Re was raised by her three sisters in a small apartment above the tavern they owned. The Buchanans lived together a number of years before they married. During this time they moved around the country in search of better jobs. Andrew reflects, "I had no intention of marrying. . . . I didn't expect to associate myself with a girl who I thought would want children. . . . If I had a boy and a girl, I would [have been] tickled to death. Now there are these other children. . . . God bless us all." Betty Re was working in her sister's tavern when she met Andrew. She recalls that he was a "neat looking fellow . . . always quiet. Off to himself reading or something like that."

They do not generally complain about their marriage. The major problem for them both has been economic. Betty Re muses:

> I wish that I had more money. But we've had the necessary things. I wouldn't say it was a strict religious home, but I have gone to the church, and I've always had a clean home and I've always had plenty of food, and plenty of company.

Betty Re feels that she and her husband have "always gotten along, like the same things . . . reading, sports, just everything the same. There's one thing I don't like; you couldn't get me to go back with him to school." In point of fact, they have very little in common and have gotten along only so long as they keep their activities quite separate.

Married life for Andrew is a mixture of happiness and severe depression. In the midst of so many children who generally speak well of him and treat him with a modicum of respect, he feels very much alone. He laments that his wife really runs the family and his kids really do not respect him, and yet they profess to have a workable agreement to divide the household chores and the household income in a manner relatively satisfactory to both. In point of fact, however, the way in which the distribution of funds and labor is accomplished is quite different from their verbal agreements. Betty Re adds to her household funds by pawning articles Andrew has saved for out of his disability checks, forcing him to redeem them whenever he can. He has, nevertheless, managed to accumulate a bank account of several hundred dollars which he guards suspiciously. He, on the other hand, manages her aggressiveness toward numerous agencies with which the family interacts. He maintains status within the family as a "thinking man," while his wife is the doer."

The most pronounced aspect of this marriage is their "working agreement." She is allowed to indulge her desire for beer, for example, and he his desire for books. She claims he has told her:

> "Now dear, you go buy whatever you want to buy. No matter if it is the last dollar we have in the house and you need beer, you go and get it." That's what I do and I in turn don't care for books. He likes books. He gets what books and typewriters and things like that he wants for his office [bedroom].

This agreement extends to most of their other activities as well, including a most unusual arrangement whereby Betty Re stays home and

Andrew goes out with his "stepdaughter" Tilly and her boyfriend on Friday nights and drinks. Andrew says, "Honey, I'm going out with Tilly tonight." She replies, "You go right ahead. I just have to go to bed, I'm too tired." This has occurred more or less regularly since Betty Re has been working.

Furthermore, they do not like each other's friends. Betty Re would have more company than Andrew feels necessary and he retorts:

> You take my wife has some friends, they come home to have a good time. "I got some beer. I got some sherry," [she says]. They set down at the table. I don't like them people. *They are her friends, not mine*. I don't have a definite reason to hate them. I just don't care for them.

Their relationship has not been smooth. They have been able to remain together for a little over seventeen years primarily because they have agreed to get out of each other's way whenever possible and because they have both been willing to assume responsibility for the upkeep of the family. She has been willing to work when he became disabled and he, likewise, has been willing to assume the major cooking responsibilities. They are thus functionally interdependent, but are building a reservoir of hostility and suspicion between them.

When they do interact with each other, there is rarely conflict. Once, however, after a trip east, Andrew and his wife were sitting in the dining room while he told of his experience. As he talked of the bus trip, Betty Re tried to interject from time to time in anticipation of the next stop. He became quite angry with her and said in a firm but subdued manner: "Honey, the bus didn't travel that way. You're going to try to tell me what it looks like. I was the one that took the trip." While this is about the upper limit of the anger expressed in the presence of non-family members, one has the feeling that it is always just below the surface. It is a rare occasion when the Buchanans are both in the same conversation.

Andrew takes pride in the fact that neither his wife nor his children can accuse him of "cutting out" with other women. He feels that in this regard at least he is setting them a good example. He claims that his wife knows that he is not cutting out because she knows he is not at this time interested in that aspect of life. In the past he has found that there are too many troubles connected with other women. Now he says he finds them too demanding economically, socially (too difficult to keep mistress and wife separated), and sexually ("they slaughter you").

The Fraziers

The Fraziers are the least urbanized of the families under consideration, having been in the city only a little over seven years. They have been married twenty years and are the only family wherein the father is younger than the mother. He is thirty-seven, she is forty. Because of the illiteracy of the parents and their fear of the streets, the family spends most of its time inside the small row apartment it has rented in the heart of the city, the last of the five residences they have moved into during the past two years. From this security it views the world largely through the eyes, ears, and mind of its oldest child, Richard. His ability is both a source of comfort and great concern for them.

They met and married in the South. "I seen her at a tavern (they call them a *juke* house down in Mississippi) one night there in town so I talked to her. She didn't talk right so I got up that Sunday morning and went up to her house. She was a nice girl. We come to like one another." Mae Apple had known Lester for a long time before they started courting. They courted two weeks and then married. She complains that she never knew much about courting because her mother was "too strict" and wouldn't let her out of the house. "She'd be courting, but she wouldn't let us court." Her mother was "cutting out" on her stepfather. Mae Apple was an "outsider," and despite her mother's strictness managed to bear one child "outside" when she was nineteen. The child never lived with the Fraziers and now Mae Apple doesn't know the name of her daughter's husband or child. She was not pregnant when she married.

The marriage took place in Lester's home. "You know how people is in the country. They just marry and it's all over with. They don't do like people do here." They were not even required to have a blood test. Immediately after they married, they moved in with *his father* for a couple of weeks. After that they lived on their own.

Both agree that married life has been good to them. Lester remarks, "It's only one thing. I just couldn't take care of my family the way I wanted to cause I couldn't get the type of work. . . ." His wife is ". . . a nice girl. As long as me and her been married I wouldn't want no better wife." Mae Apple agrees, "I've been happy every since I've been with him." This couple has the most positive attitude toward their relationship of any of those visited.

For both Fraziers "cutting out" is unheard of. Lester puts it this way:

> That's not right. Somebody is wrong. . . . I'll tell you, take myself. I ain't no dead old man. That's something that don't worry my mind to be running out in the street. That don't make no sense to think about no woman out in the street cause I ain't got nothing to give 'em. They don't want nothing but money. If you got some money all right. If you ain't got no money you are in bad shape. What little I've got I can use and some more besides it. If you see me, you see my woman.

Mae Apple does not cross Lester. She follows his lead in such matters as the decision to move to the city or to buy a new car, and gives him equal say in money matters of all sorts. She runs the house with the help of her girls. Richard is a source of tension because he does not want to do chores around the house. He would rather help out by using his brain and doesn't want to be seen "junking it" with his father to supplement the family income, which is now mainly welfare since his father's heart attack enabled him to draw disability checks. His wife's ADC combines to give them an income of $4,896 for a family of eleven. This is not supplemented by any illegitimate sources of income.

Mae Apple works with her girls. Usually they cooperate with her and do their work. They often do more and wait upon her, bringing her her slippers and lighting her cigarettes. She wears a heavy golden chain attached to her glasses that permits them to hang down about her neck when not in use. When indoors she usually wears brightly colored slacks and blouses occasionally topped off with a Jamaican straw hat not intended to give the comic impression that it does. Mae Apple is the lady of the house, her girls are ladies-in-waiting.

As the lady of the house, she would like to oversee its upkeep and not do any of the work. This she can do only up to a point. Her daughters sweep and clean, wash dishes, make their beds, but if she wants the job done right and the floors spotless she has to go over the work herself. Lester helps her in this occasionally, but normally he is resting when around the house.

The Fraziers—particularly Lester—believe that parents control their children best by setting a good example for them. When the parents behave, the children have nothing "over them" to use as an excuse for their own misconduct:

> Well I consider myself a good father to my kids. I can't get no one who will speak nard against me. You've got to be good to your children for them to treat you right. If you ain't good to them they [won't] speak good about you. I ain't got none who will speak slack about me. They give me a good name before anybody. I have heard lots of people ask them, "How is your daddy?" They say, "My daddy is good to me." Daddy will turn his pockets out for them because I love them.

He feels that his parents set him a good example:

> I had a good mother and father. I ain't never known nothing wrong. I ain't never seen nothing wrong in my eyesight. They would teach us to go to church and teach us how to treat people. They never teach us nothing wrong. So therefore, I can't say nothing but a good mother and father teach you that.

And when he was asked why some parents have trouble raising their children so that they will mind, he replied:

> Well I'll tell you, it's a very few kids I've seen now that come up like I come up. 'Cause I have been to lots of houses and it's some mighty dim things they teach their children. Some people got kids that will do just like they tell them, and some got kids that will do the wrong thing from what they tell them. I have noticed this. I have been to lots of houses and I've seen some pretty rough deals with kids. I'll tell you what that come from. That comes from mother and daddy. If you do any and everything over your child you can't expect no better, can you? Not if you let your child do them kind of things.
>
> . . . [If] me and my wife do any and everything over these children, the first thing they'll say is, "Mama, you and daddy you all do it." It ain't nothing for us to say. Now what can we

> say? We can't say nothing. . . . If your child can't say they seen you doing this or that you're bound to be holding a good program for them. I don't let my children see me do no things wrong. Not one thing. I'm not playing. I ain't got none that can tell you that today. They ain't never seen daddy come in here drunk, cussing, clowning or nothing. They'll tell you that right now. Daddy is going to come in here as he leaves. . . . I ain't going to come in here drunk and beating my wife over my kids. Of course I don't jump on her and beat her no how.

Lester and Mae Apple are thus in a difficult position *vis-à-vis* their children, particularly their oldest boy Richard. They do their best to be good parents to their children; they do not behave in the way they know many parents do (drinking and cussing and stepping out on each other). In other words, they provide a quite adequate model for what is acceptable traditional behavior—they are "respectable." But they cannot help their children adapt to the ways of the city. If anything, they are a hindrance because of their educational and cultural handicaps and their fear of city ways. Yet, despite the handicaps, Lester is very well thought of in his family and his children are well behaved. The Frazier family is in fact a warm, intimate shelter from the harsh realities of the street. If they had the earning capacity to become upwardly mobile legitimately, such a family would closely approximate the working-class nuclear family. Ironically, however, their conception of morality is a handicap in teaching the children how to cope with the world in which they find themselves. Thus, they obtain a degree of intimacy at the expense of acquiring effective survival techniques.

A TYPOLOGY OF MALE MARGINALITY IN COMPLETE FAMILIES

The Indiscreet "Free Man"

The most marginal type of father suggested by these data is what might be called the indiscreet free man. What is apparent in his relationship to his family is a split in allegiance between his legitimate family and one or more "illegitimate" families. This outside interest is continually paraded before his wife and family either in a constant, chiding reference to the "other woman" or by the deliberate engineering of an encounter with her. His interests outside the family are reflected in his spending on behalf of the other woman and, if he has had children by her, a regular amount may be set aside each month in their behalf—regardless of whether or not the court has intervened. More commonly he will buy shoes, clothing, and gifts for them from time to time. Such a father's interests reverberate upon his children, creating an intensified kind of sibling rivalry with his "outside" children, who, in some instances, are known personally by his legitimate children. Life within such families is thus one of constant conflict and bickering. That they stay intact at all is probably related to (1) the advancing age of the wife, which, combined with her many children, makes her less and less attractive to other men and more and more destined to head a household should her husband leave; (2) her continuing hope that he will reform his ways; and (3) his positive, if sometimes sporadic, contributions in support and affection to his family. Two families fit this type: the Pattersons and the Billits.

The Discreet "Free Man"

In contrast to the indiscreet free man, the discreet man's "cutting out" is clearly a secondary concern which he does not use to antagonize his wife and children. As a result, his indiscretions are largely known only to himself, or, if known by his wife, are "understood," and both partners are likely to admit "we get along well enough." His relationship to his children is not particularly impaired as a result of his interest outside the home, and they often look upon him as an ideal father. Typically, just as he is able to cover up or minimize his activities with other women, so also is he able to carry on deviant activities such as gambling or pimping without these appreciably interfering with his home life. Knowledge of such activity may in fact provide a means of legitimating his authority over his children, who tend to see him as being a smart man able to cope with his environment, if not legitimately, then, when necessary, illegitimately.

Such families give a strong first impression of stability. Two families fit this type: the Washingtons and the Buchanans.

The Traditional Monogamous Type

The last type can be labeled the traditional monogamous type of father because he is proud of the fact that he is able to say, "If you see me, you see my woman." This type, although apparently rare in fact, is reflected in numerous references in the data to the effect that it is desirable. In such a family the father does not cut out, and if he has had any children "outside," they are the result of his youthful indiscretions and not a result of his violation of monogamous marriage. His home and family are his major concerns and receive his constant attention. Typically such a father will have good relationships with his children and high status in the family regardless of his ability to earn a living. Only one family fits this type: the Fraziers.

THE FIVE "INCOMPLETE" FAMILIES

Because marriage is a difficult contract to honor under the conditions of ghetto existence, it is not surprising that many break up. In the project 55 per cent of the households were headed by women. Most of these were women who had previously been married. In the case of the five incomplete families, the marriages failed after children had been born to the couples, and the mothers were left with the responsibility for their care. With poor education, few skills, and little in the way of family resources to draw upon, this means that "going on welfare" is a decided possibility. In the project this is the choice taken by the majority.

However, welfare (in the form of Aid to Families with Dependent Children, Veteran's pension if the husband was a veteran, or Social Security benefits) is rarely enough to enable a family to live with any comforts, most often sustaining them at a very minimal level. All of the mothers now heading families have been on ADC at one time or another. Four of them still are.

The problem of providing for their families is frequently combined with the search for a dependable man who might eventually become a husband. The role played by the boyfriend in such a context is thus quite varied. He may be wholly or largely exploitive of the relationship, like the pimp, or he may be as supportive as is possible in the situation and seek a familial relationship with his woman and her family. The analysis continues with a brief discussion of the arrangements made by the five women now heading households.

Lilly Parvin

Lilly Parvin knew her husband from childhood. She never was very "boy crazy" and had only one boyfriend before she met her husband. This boyfriend she remembers as a very religious boy who used to discuss the Bible with her mother. She met him when she was fourteen. He, in the fashion of all lovers, asked her to marry, and she said yes. But he went overseas to Korea and she lost contact with him. Prior to his last letter, however, she had already turned to a childhood friend, D. J.. Although her religious convictions and her upbringing were against premarital sexual relations, she entered marriage at the age of twenty-one already five months pregnant. They were married by a justice of the peace across the state line and shortly after marriage went to live in another state while her husband was in the Army. Their marriage lasted about seven years. His increasing "cutting out" forced her to return home to stay with her father more and more often before he finally dropped her and her six children off on a street corner near her father's house. He has not been heard from since.

Lilly remembers her marriage with mixed emotions. At first it was very happy, but then it fell apart. Since then life has been very difficult:

> I've had such a hard time, I haven't had time to miss him since *I left him.* I don't know what love is anyway. Guess I'm different. . . . I haven't been happy in a long time. . . . My sister says we didn't used to get along, but we used to get along. We had some good times together. When we first started out we used to go places. We'd go to the beach, drive-ins . . . watch people at the

> Speedway, go to the carnival. Me and him and the kids got along pretty nice.

Since she has been alone she has suffered increasing mental incapacitation and most of the time feels depressed, quite threatened, and totally a failure. She wants nothing more to do with men, despite the fact that a male friend of her brother-in-law's has been able to force his affections on her on several occasions. She flatly states, "I don't want to get married again. I'm on welfare now. I don't need a husband."

Leona Wards

Leona Wards met all her boyfriends through the church where her uncle preached. She met her first boyfriend when she was fifteen, but the only courting they did was in the nature of his visiting her at home. "We never went out." That relationship lasted about eight months, and when she was sixteen she met her husband, who drove for a local undertaker. At seventeen she married. She claims, "My husband didn't know whether I was a woman or a man until after he married me. I never did have no relationship with him. . . . My sister was the same way . . . [she] never had no man but her husband." She adds: "That's the way you're supposed to be reared, and that's the way you're supposed to be reared today. That's what I tell my girls." The aunt by whom she was reared did not approve of the wedding, but saw to it that her niece was married in church.

> I had a *wedding* when I married him and I believe in it right today. When I married I was in white satin. . . . Anytime I look in the paper and see a girl with a gown cut off, short sleeves and marrying, she's no virgin. A virgin marries when you see nothing but a very little bit of her neck.

Shortly after they were married, she discovered through a friend that her husband had been "cutting out" on her. She stayed with him over fourteen years. Finally she consulted a marriage counselor and claims she took the professional's advice and left her husband, after having borne him four children. This occurred in 1948, and since that time she has given birth to three more children by a boyfriend, a relationship to be discussed in some detail in a following section.

Dorothy Brown

Dorothy Brown has been married twice and is now separated from her second husband. Prior to her first marriage she gave birth to her first child, Ann, when she was seventeen. She married her first husband at twenty-five, rather on the late side by community standards. She describes her first husband as "one of the meanest niggers I have ever known in my life. . . . He was a tight and overbearing man, all the nine years I knew him. He would beat me. . . . My second husband, he didn't beat me but he disappointed me." Dorothy married her first husband, whom she had known for some time, "to get out on [her] own. I didn't want to walk out of the house, 'cause I figured when I was at home I was working too hard."

Her second husband disappointed her by going out with her best friend and requesting, after a lengthy affair, that this friend be allowed to come and live with them. Dorothy left home and came to the city. Now she is wary of all men:

> Six years I ain't had nobody. . . . Well, I guess some of it is my fault [but] I'm afraid to trust men. I done been mistreated by two. . . . I have had men to ask me to be their girlfriend, woman or wife, but I'm absolutely scared. *I don't know if I am getting a right somebody or a wrong somebody.* . . . I know a fellow, he's been begging for the last six months for me to be his woman or his wife. I still don't know how it would turn out. I hate to be hurt again a third time.

This fellow is her present boyfriend, whom she is testing. She finally told him that she would be his woman for a while in order to find out what kind of man he really is.

Tilly Handy

The information about Tilly Handy is somewhat contradictory. There is strong insinuation that she has had several children by men to whom she has not been married. Her half-brother Gerald tells about one of her experiences with a married man.

> . . . My sister she and her husband got separated and she was going with a man, and my mother, she knew the man and knew that he was married. She told my sister and . . . she wouldn't give him up. They was in the house one day and his wife ran over and started fussing at him and he got mad and they started fighting and so that was a lesson for my sister.

Her mother and "stepfather," the Buchanans, talk about her as the *black sheep* of the family (although she is always welcome at their home). They imply that she has been very promiscuous and has borne several children "outside" as a result. But she herself claims not to have borne any children outside of marriage. She admits having been pregnant before her first marriage: "When my mother told me I was pregnant, he said he would marry me." Tilly didn't know where babies came from at the age of fourteen when she first became pregnant. Her first husband was a high school friend known to the family. Her mother, Betty Re, made the arrangements (as she was to do many years later in the cases of Tilly's half-siblings, Gerald and Della). "After my mother told me I was pregnant, [she] told his mother and his mother told him to marry. So we did and we lived together until Irving [the next baby born to them] was ten years old." Thus they remained married about eleven years, although Tilly almost immediately rejected her husband. "I just didn't want to see him after what he had did. . . . I felt he had did me wrong and I shouldn't have been this way." Her first delivery was by Caesarean section.

When her first husband came back from the Army, "he was a different man. He didn't want to work. He just wanted to be in the poolroom all day. As to supporting his family he didn't want to do it. I guess he figured *his mother* would take care of them. *She did for two years.*" While her husband was in the Army she stayed with her mother and stepfather, moving out to live with her husband a while and then returning "home." Thus it seems that this marriage was arranged and largely sustained by the efforts of both mothers. The separation came three weeks after he returned from the Army. Undoubtedly the stay in the Army was a factor in bringing it about. A divorce was obtained shortly afterward. It took place out of court: "they just agreed between two lawyers." Tilly did not ask for alimony, "I didn't want anything because I was working . . . as a nurse."

Her second marriage lasted about two years. "I didn't know that he was an alcoholic. I didn't know that. I found out two hours later after we were married." She married shortly after having met her second husband, even before he had an opportunity to meet her children or her parents. She knew very little about him. The marriage was impossible:

> I told him I had the two kids and he tried to get along with them. But he hit them and that made me fret. I told him don't hit the kids and he kept on. I didn't know he drank this heavy and when I found out it got on my nerves because his drinking everyday wouldn't go right.

He beat her on their wedding night and sent her to the hospital as the result of a beating he inflicted during the first week of their marriage. The marriage ended as swiftly as it began. "One Saturday he just got up and walked away. I went to him and talked to him and he said no, he wasn't coming back. I just said, 'You walked off on me, I didn't leave you.' "

She had three children by her first husband and six by her second, and all the children see their fathers regularly. The older children visit their father about once a week, but because of her fear of her second husband's drinking, Tilly will not allow her younger children to visit him. He comes by about every two months. Both pay some child support for their children, even though her first husband has remarried and has children by his second wife. Before she married her second husband, Tilly had a steady boyfriend. After her separation she came back to him and they have been going together a total of about eleven years.

Like Dorothy, Tilly does not feel that she is ready for marriage again, but she has decided that the way in which she will know a good man the next time is by the way he treats her children. "If he don't love your kids, he don't love you."

Ethyl Perry

Ethyl Perry, the last of the women heading families in our sample, married a childhood friend when she was fifteen. Her mother had her "outside" after her first marriage, and Ethyl never knew that her stepfather was not her real father until her older sister told her. Her stepfather left to live with another woman shortly after Ethyl's marriage, and her mother never remarried but continued to live with a boyfriend.

Ethyl's marriage came about under a double pressure. She had become pregnant by the father of the boy she was going with, but this man suddenly had to leave town because of some trouble with a white man. He left not knowing that Ethyl was carrying his child. She, in the meantime, had convinced herself that her boyfriend would marry her if she became pregnant and initiated "relations" with him. They married and he never found out until later that Mary was his father's child. Ethyl feels that despite this inauspicious beginning the first years of her marriage were good ones. Her husband was particularly proud when she gave birth to a son in the second year of their marriage. After the third child came, however, he seemed to lose interest. "Then he started drinking and staying away from home. . . . He was real cruel. He like to fight and I didn't. . . . We'd fight sometimes two or three times a week. . . . I put up with that for almost two years. Then I left and I was too proud to go back." She is the only unmarried woman to express regret over her separation, even though now she has other interests. "I miss him sometimes, you know. I think about him I guess . . . just in a small way." They had been married six years.

Since coming to the city in 1959, Ethyl has had a series of boyfriends and the details of these relationships will be discussed in the following section.

SUMMARY OF THE MARITAL EXPERIENCE OF FEMALE HOUSEHOLD HEADS

All of the three "shotgun" marriages that occurred are now terminated by separation or divorce. The only other instance of a marriage preceding a first birth (not a "shotgun") is likewise terminated. The remaining woman now heading a household had her first child before marriage, but the marriage itself was not the result of pregnancy. Four of the five women now heading households thus married under pressure of some sort, be it Dorothy Brown's strong desire to get out on her own, Tilly Handy's mother's insistence that she marry in order to stop disgracing the family, or the pressure of "outside" children, with or without parental intervention.

The complaints against the former husbands are amazingly consistent. All five complain of other women: "He seemed to be all right at first but then he began cutting out." Nonsupport was charged in two instances, fights in which the woman was beaten occur in four cases, and drinking problems in three.[3] The right to beat a wife seems to be accepted as a normal right of a man who "has papers" on a woman. Stanley Billit states this explicitly when he remarks, "['Cause] that's a man's wife he can do what he wants to her. If he wants to whip her he can whip her," and it is certainly implied in the advice Alliena Billit received from her mother, "If you don't think you can just lay down and let that man walk all over you, don't you get married."

A man is overbearing even to the point of physical abuse, a woman

[3] The distribution of reasons given for disruption of a marriage in our sample survey is as follows:

Sexual infidelity	40%
Husband wouldn't support her	20
Husband lost job, couldn't find another	3
One partner too immature	17
Husband drank excessively	15
Husband cruel, beat her	15
Husband gambled too much	7
Husband in jail	3
Unspecified infidelity	22
Husband just deserted, no reason	8

Source: Lee Rainwater, "The Problem of Lower Class Culture and Poverty War Strategy" (St. Louis: The Social Science Institute, Washington University, Occasional Paper No. 34, 1967), p. 31.

This represents the response of sixty women whose marriages were disrupted by separation or divorce. Obviously a woman could give more than one reason for the disruption. It is clear that the responses from the five women in this study reflect similar patterns.

forbears and endures. A *good* man doesn't do such things to his wife, but so many do that a good man is seen as the exception. Thus, all of the women in this group are very much afraid of marriage because no matter how good a man might seem before marriage, after he "has papers" on you he might well change. In such a situation the role of the boyfriend becomes an important way of testing a man as well as a means of support and a source of companionship.

THE ROLE OF THE BOYFRIEND

The importance of the boyfriend's role becomes apparent when one realizes that four of the five women who are now heading households receive support from boyfriends. The amount of support and the type of relationship that exists vary considerably and suggest a typology consisting of four different roles which a boyfriend may play and for which there is some support from segments of this population. These types are: the quasi-father, the supportive biological father, the supportive companion, and the pimp. The image of the pimp has dominated the literature thus far.[4] In this relationship the male is largely exploitive.

However, there is also in the literature some evidence that these nonmarital liaisons between men and women of the Negro lower class are more stable than is commonly acknowledged. In *Blackways of Kent,* Lewis mentions in passing that "gifts and some degree of support from the male are taken for granted and freely discussed. There is some informal ranking of men on a basis of the regularity and amount of gifts or support." [5] In this section fuller documentation of this support in nonmarital liaisons will be presented. In so doing, we

[4] For some discussion of this facet of the boyfriend's role, see in particular the following: John Dollard, *Caste and Class in a Southern Town,* 2nd ed. (New Haven: Yale University Press, 1939), pp. 160–61; Kenneth Clark, *Dark Ghetto* (New York: Harper & Row, Publishers, 1965), pp. 67–80; E. Franklin Frazier, *The Negro in the United States* (Chicago: University of Chicago Press, 1960), p. 214; Sinclair Drake and Horace Clayton, *Black Metropolis* (New York: Harcourt, Brace & World, Inc., 1945), pp. 570 ff.; and Abraham Kardiner and Lionel Ovesey, *Mark of Oppression* (New York: Meridian Books, 1962), pp. 69–70.

[5] Hylan Lewis, *Blackways of Kent* (Chapel Hill: University of North Carolina Press, 1961), p. 84. See also E. Franklin Frazier, *op. cit.,* p. 215, and Drake and Cayton, *loc. cit.*

hope to make it apparent that the lower-class Negro man contributes to the welfare of his woman more than is commonly acknowledged, and plays an important role of surrogate father to her children.

The Quasi-Father

The distinguishing marks of the quasi-father are that (1) he supports the family regularly over long periods of time (eleven years is the longest known, though this was interrupted by a short marriage; five years is the longest consecutive time known at present). Often he will go with his woman to the store and buy her week's food. (2) His concern extends directly to her children as well. He will give them allowances or spending money, attempt more or less successfully to discipline them, and will take them out to the park, to the movies, or to other places for entertainment. (3) He frequently visits the family during the week, and may or may not reside with them in the project—usually not. The relationship is not ordinarily conducted clandestinely, but in full knowledge of kin on both sides—particularly the parents, if they reside in the same city with the couple. In return for this he receives (1) his meals (some or all if residing with the family); (2) washing and ironing; (3) sexual satisfaction, and (4) *familial companionship*. In short, he seems to be bargaining for more than just a woman in seeking intimacy in the context of a family. To illustrate let us take the example of Jay and Ethyl.

Ethyl Perry (thirty-three) went with Jay (twenty-four) for over five years. During that time he took her out, bought her the majority of her furniture, and supplied her with fifteen to twenty dollars per week, usually by means of buying her week's food. In addition his family contributed several pieces of furniture and invited Ethyl over for meals on occasion. None of her six children is his. Ethyl describes Jay as a "nice person . . . kind-hearted" and by this she means that, ". . . he believes in survival for me and my family, me and my kids. He don't mind sharing with my youngsters. If I ask him for a helping hand, he don't seem to mind that. The only part of it is that I dislike his drinking." It's not the drinking as such that Ethyl dislikes, but the man Jay becomes when he drinks. He becomes angry and quick tempered, but has yet to beat Ethyl when in such a state.

Jay's concern for Ethyl's children is expressed in various ways.

As Dovie, Ethyl's fifteen-year-old daughter, sees Jay, he tends to be bossy. "He be all right sometimes but he drinks and that's the reason I don't like him. . . . He tries to boss people. Like if my boyfriends come over here he be saying I can't have no company." But Mary, her eighteen-year-old daughter, revealed that Jay gave her a small washing machine for her baby's diapers. She said, "My mother's *boyfriend* bought it. . . . It was about three days after my baby was born."

Jay's concern is expressed in other ways as well. He took the children to the movies, to the park, gave them a small allowance as spending money each week when he bought the groceries, and once, when Ethyl was sick, he took care of the youngest two for nearly a month while she was in the hospital. During the years that they were going together Jay visited the family several times a week, most frequently spending the weekend with them. He continually asked Ethyl to marry him, though Ethyl felt he was only half serious. Jay was asked why he bothered to take care of Ethyl and he replied, "That's a personal question. . . . Well, first of all I help her because I love her and we're going to get married sometime, but not just now because we can't afford it."

A second example is that of Tilly (thirty-three) and Sam (thirty-four—looks twenty-five). Tilly has been going with Sam for over eleven years—even while married to her second husband, whom she finally left for Sam. He helps the budget regularly out of his pay as a dock worker in a river barge yard. Tilly says, "Sam gives me thirty dollars a week." He has also bought several small pieces of furniture and takes her out almost every weekend. He lives just around the corner with his cousin, visits the family almost every night, and sometimes spends the night, though he usually sleeps with his cousin.

Tilly feels that Sam "treats her kids better than their daddy do. He buys them certain things [such as] clothes. He spanks them. . . . He takes them different places." She further feels that it is very important that a man treat her kids right. "If they don't care for the kids or anything then that's a bad man. . . . First he's got to love your kids before he loves you."

Her sons Richard (ten) and William (seventeen) confirm the fact that Sam is concerned about the children. Richard says, "He takes up for us when we get a whipping. . . . He tells her not to whip us this time." When asked, "Does he have pretty good control over the kids?" William replied, "They do what he say most of the time. Irvin [eighteen] don't, but the rest of them will."

They are still going together and Sam proposes marriage with some regularity, but Tilly shies away. "I think I'm better off just not having a husband. . . . I wouldn't definitely say I would get a good one. I might get a bad one. I don't want to take a chance." Even though she has known Sam since childhood, she is not certain about him. He drinks a lot but is not to her knowledge the violent type—at least he is not as a single man. Her fear is that when he "has papers on her" he might change. Her experience with her second husband taught her how quickly a man could change on her.

And so Ethyl broke up with Jay, never having seriously considered marriage while going with him and Tilly says that *maybe* in three or four years she will be ready for marriage to Sam. Marriage has not yet resulted because in both instances the family is doing better under the combined resources of welfare and the boyfriend's assistance than they could do under his wages alone, and in both instances the woman is afraid of the man's drinking behavior. In both instances the boyfriends are well known by the women's families and visit frequently with them.

Since breaking with Jay, Ethyl has been living with a new boyfriend, Raymond (twenty-nine), and says that she is seriously considering marriage to him—at least to the extent that she has decided to get a divorce. Thus, marriage may or may not be a result of a quasi-father relationship, but it does provide the context in which a woman with children is likely to make up her mind one way or another about a man. It is interesting to remember here that three of the five women still living with their husbands began their relationship "common law." Only one of the quasi-fathers at present lives with his woman.

The Supportive Biological Father

A second type of boyfriend is the supportive biological father. Here the concern of the man—and largely that of the woman also—is to support the children that they have brought into the world without seriously considering marriage to one another. In some instances the man or woman may well be married to someone else. The man's support may be voluntary, as in the case of Edward Patterson, or it may be as the result of a voluntarily signed acknowledgment that the children are his.

In the case of Leona Wards (fifty) and Larry (forty-nine), Leona was married once and had four children by her first husband. His "cutting out" and drinking led to a separation and Leona took up with Larry, who gave her three children, in ages now from eighteen to thirteen, before he married another woman a couple of years ago. He played the role of supportive biological father before he married. They had been going together for nearly *sixteen* years, though only Leona was true to the relationship. She has never remarried and claims that even now she has no boyfriend because they are too much trouble at her age, although she admits that she would enjoy a companion in her declining years.

Larry has taken the children on long trips, such as the one to Arizona in 1963, he has bought them clothes, especially at Christmas time, and has paid regularly the amount of fifteen to twenty dollars a week for their support since 1954. At that time he acknowledged that the children are his and the court fixed the amount for their support.

Leona's being true to Larry is a part of her rearing as she sees it. Her mother died in 1927 and "daddy went haywire," so she went to live with her maternal aunt and her husband, Uncle Paul—"gentle Paul"—who was a Baptist minister. Her aunt was a very strict woman and quite respectable.

Leona's marriage lasted fourteen years, and at the end she left her husband because he was undependable in his support of her and the children. While separated she met Larry, her boyfriend:

> At the time I met Larry, my first husband and I wasn't together. I met Larry through the [same] church. He asked me [to marry] and I told him not until my husband's children got off my hands and out of the way. I never wanted a stepfather over my children . . . it was something that Lewis and I have always said.

Her main departure from her rearing was having children out of wedlock, and while she loves the children, she regrets the departure:

> That's the only thing in life I didn't want—to have children without being married. I just wasn't reared like that. But *they*

> *are all by one man.* They're not by this, that one, nor the other one. They're all by one man.

Leona is proud to be able to say, "I have been by Larry as if he and I were married." But he was not true to her. She broke off their relationship by cutting him with a knife.

While it is true that Larry is legally obligated to care for his children, it is noteworthy that he claimed them as his in the first place and that he supports them in gifts over and above his legal obligations. His inability to believe that Leona was true to him, plus her reluctance to have a stepfather over her husband's children, at least one of whom has not yet left home, contributed to the factors other than economic that mitigated against their marriage—but did not prevent them from courting for sixteen years.

Most of the care that fathers give to their outside children seems to be much less regular than Larry's, but is, nevertheless, largely voluntary. Edward Patterson, for example, has three by two different women. His outside children live with their mothers, and when he gets tired of his wife he moves out and lives with Leddie B., by whom he has had two children. His legitimate children complain that when he goes to visit one of the outsiders, he gives her and her siblings more money for spending than he gives his legitimate children. His wife protests that he stole their TV set and gave it to the mother of one of these children, and his son claims that when he returned to his home in the country recently, he bought several dresses for his outside child living there. Mr. Patterson will not speak of these outsiders and keeps his money matters to himself. His wife has opened letters from the mothers of these children requesting regular support, but does not know if he is giving only to them. She believes that he spends most of the $406 a month take-home pay he earns from his job on these women and their children.

The Supportive Companion

A less durable relationship exists in the case of the "supportive companion" who "keeps a woman." Here the concern of the male is mainly to have a good time with a clean woman. The concern of the woman is for support and companionship. Such a relationship is not to be confused with prostitution, for it is not a mere matter of a business transaction but a search for intimacy on both parts, a search conducted in the context of severe economic and emotional handicaps. In this community such a relationship is likely to occur between an older man (late twenties, early thirties) and a younger woman (early twenties, teens) who has had children outside of wedlock.

In such a relationship, the man rarely keeps the woman in her own apartment, as would be the case in more solvent circumstances, where the woman is usually single and without children. Rather, he provides a regular "weekend away" at his apartment or other suitable place where they can be together away from the children. He takes her out, provides her with spending money and a good time. Should she conceive a child, he is least likely of all types to want to assume support of the child. Responsibility is what he is trying to avoid.

The example of Madeline (sixteen) and Jerry (twenty-three) is a case in point. They knew each other about a year during 1959–1960. Madeline had already had two children by two other men. Jerry came by for dinner occasionally, but usually he made the weekend scene at a motel apartment he rented for the occasion. When Friday came round, he would give Madeline money which she often turned into dresses or other items to enhance her appearance. Madeline says, "Jerry's not like a lot of men that you find. A lot of men, if they do something for you they feel they own you." Jerry gave her "fifteen or twenty dollars, sometimes more" each week and had keys to a two-room kitchenette for the weekend. Madeline says, "We were always together [on the weekend]. Where I went he usually went, where he went I went. We'd go to the apartment and everything. But lots of times we would go and just watch TV or sit and talk or have a drink or something. Then we would go—especially in the summertime—we'd go there because they had air conditioning."

The Pimp

As we have indicated in Chapter 3, the pimp is characteristic of the young man of the street who lives off the labors of prostitutes or off women who are able to earn their own way through wages or welfare. He is kept by his woman and dresses like a dandy. None of the women living in broken homes has had a pimp, but Andrew

Buchanan claims he was one as a youth. The pimp relationship may be, for the man at least, quite often a *pre*marital experience and for that reason it was treated in the section "Coming Up as a Boy."

Speculation on Extensiveness and Relationship in Time

While there is no accurate measure of the prevalence of these four types of boyfriends, the data are suggestive. The pimp is the most talked about male-female nonmarital relationship in the literature. These data, however, suggest that it is not as prevalent in the project as is commonly assumed. It is possible that pimping may be more or less restricted to the younger men and may phase out into less exploitive relationships with females as the men grow older. Therefore, the frequency of the pimping relationship may well be exaggerated, since the younger men tend to be more vocal about their exploits, and the older men who now view such activity with a certain resentment may bewail the fact that "things used to be much better."

A man may play one or more boyfriend roles in his life. We can thus see these types as phases in a developmental sequence. The pimp is an early role of the young man of the street who would rather "live sweet" than work, or who has found that his value on the love market is greater than it is on the labor market. The data suggest that such a relationship is quite likely to terminate when the man reaches his mid-thirties. He may then decide to marry the woman he has pimped off because by then he has had one or more children by her, or because he is, after having sown his wild oats, seeking now a more intimate and lasting relationship. If he does marry her, then he comes under the norm that it is "unfair" to pimp off a woman you are married to.

No one, however, has gone from a pimping relationship directly to marriage with the same woman. In the case of Edward Patterson, who pimped off several women for several years before marriage, a quasi-father relationship was entered into with another woman for four or five years before he married her as the result of an unwanted pregnancy. This marriage has lasted nineteen years.

The quasi-fathers are in their late twenties or early thirties, and in one of the three instances, marriage is actively sought by the woman. In the other two the males are still being tested. This opportunity to get to know a man under near familial situations is a boon to these women, who have been disappointed in marriage one or more times. He can prove that he is a good provider and a gentle, "good" man. Not all quasi-father relationships terminate in marriage.

The supportive companion is, if the data from these inferences are correct, more likely to be the relationship that exists between an older man (late twenties or early thirties) and a younger woman (late teens, early twenties). It may be an alternative for a rejected quasi-father, who sought but could not obtain marriage, and whose income is stable enough to permit such indulgence. Finally, most men can play, if they so desire, the role of supportive biological father throughout most of their lives, since almost every male has had at least one child outside of wedlock. For some who never marry, this may be the extent to which their craving for familial companionship is expressed—the occasional gift to an illegitimate child.

A Complete Typology of Male Marginality

A simple resolution of the relationship between the typology of marginality developed for fathers in complete families and the one just concluded in regard to the boyfriends could be gained by simply extending the scale for married men to include those unmarried, in the order of their perceived marginality from the monogamous father to the pimp. This, however, places too much weight on the matter of "papers," and tends to support the simplistic argument that any father is better than no father at all. Such is not the case.

On the contrary, the data indicate that the quasi-father relationships are at least equal to, if not better than, the indiscreet free man type. The tensions in the households where the husband-father is indiscreetly cutting out are more numerous and pronounced than in households where there are quasi-fathers. The fact that the indiscreet free men are able, if they are working and not receiving disability, to provide more for the family materially might give them the edge over the quasi-fathers. However, when it is remembered that the quasi-fathers contribute on the average more money to the household than a man on disability is likely to be able to, the value of the boyfriend's role increases and the economic pressures against marriage seem larger.

For this small sample, then, the ranking would be—in order of increasing marginality:

1) Monogamous father
2) Discreet free man
3) Indiscreet free man/quasi-father
4) Supportive biological father
5) Supportive companion
6) Pimp

Conclusions

The data suggest:

1. Any father is not necessarily better than no father at all. The indiscreet free man creates much more conflict in his household than the quasi-father, and his economic contributions may not be much larger.

2. The most effective father for ghetto youths, given a low probability of upward mobility, is the discreet free man, who both maintains a stable household and is able to train his children in effective if sometimes illicit techniques for coping with their world as they find it.

3. Ironically, the father who most favorably conforms to middle-class perceptions of what is desirable paternal behavior and is also unlikely to move upward handicaps his children because he is unwilling or unable to teach them such coping skills. If, as is all too likely, these children cannot move out of the ghetto, they become marginal to two worlds, unable to really participate in either.

4. Training children by example rather than precept is the preferred mode of socialization, but is perceived as more effective by those fathers adhering to the monogamous tradition because they feel that their children have less "over them."

5. Some men, perhaps most at some time in their lives, assume a very responsible "quasi-father" role *vis-à-vis* their woman and her

children. They seem to spend a considerable portion of their lives bargaining for a familial relationship, the major obstacle to which seems to be a limited income that cannot equal the combined resources of their present jobs plus their woman's welfare check.

6. The quasi-father role provides the women, who have been hurt in previous marriages, an opportunity to test their men by the adage, "love my children before you love me" before entering again into marriage.

7. Aside from this relationship, there are other situations in which the men play a more supportive role than is generally acknowledged. Such are the cases of the supportive biological father and the supportive companion. In such roles the man also provides a male role model for her children, the value of which has not been discussed in the literature.

8. Such male support in the lower-class life—in situations where it is extremely difficult to render such assistance—argues for the view that improved income and job opportunities for the lower-class Negro male will indeed result in more of these relationships terminating in marriages and, in general, more stability in family life.

Chapter 5

The Problem with "Papers"[1]

It would be a serious mistake to leave the impression that the problems of the Negro lower class derive mainly from patterns of agonistic sexual development and broken unstable families.[2] Yet this is one possible interpretation of the data thus far presented. Such factors do present problems for project residents, as well as esoteric material for researchers and relished tidbits for white racists. In all probability these factors do contribute to the intergenerational transmission of poverty.[3] But these patterns of socialization arise in the context of a racist society which has placed many constraints upon project dwellers that reduce their chances of mobility both vertically up the status ladder and horizontally away from the ghetto.[4] These constraints help

[1] Data in this chapter are drawn from several families who were not included in the original ten described in Chapter 1 because they were known less well, but who are here able to provide additional perspectives on the problems of marriage.

[2] This line of thought has been made quite prominent by the controversy raging around the U.S. Department of Labor, *The Negro Family: The Case for National Action* (Washington, D.C.: The U.S. Government Printing Office, 1965).

[3] See Charles Willie, "Intergenerational Poverty" (paper presented at The Pennsylvania State University, June 1968). Willie argues, however, that such personal factors are more likely to account for poverty among *white* families than among nonwhite.

[4] A report based on the mid-decade census survey by the U.S. Department of Labor, *Current Population Reports,* Series P–23, No. 24, "Social and Economic Conditions of Negroes in the United States" (Washington, D.C.: The U.S. Government Printing Office, 1967), indicates that in eight of twelve cities surveyed the indices of residential segregation over the period 1960–1965 point to increasing segregation. This continues a trend of increasing segregation since World War II. Another report drawn upon this census data by the Bureau of the Census, *Current Population Reports,* Series P–20, No. 54, "The Extent of Poverty in the United States, 1959–1966" (Washington, D.C.: The U.S. Government Printing Office, 1968), shows that the distribution of income in the United States has not changed appreciably since World War II, and that, although the "white and nonwhite have shared in the gains recorded by the nation in its

create the feelings of hopelessness, powerlessness, and despair that pervade ghetto life. They can now be taken more fully into account by placing these couples more firmly in their milieu.

Why is lifelong monogamous marriage so difficult in the ghetto? There are many possible answers to this question, the most important of which derive from the economic handicaps faced by the man because he is poorly educated, poorly trained, and black. It is thus very difficult for him to provide for his wife and family and maintain his status in their eyes.[5] A second group of answers derive from the open temptations of the street and its way of life, in which every person is viewed as a potential object of conquest and manipulation. Street life[6] not only advocates exploitive relationships between the sexes but encourages alternative conceptions of the ideal marriage that conflict with monogamy viewed normally as including exclusive sexual rights. A third kind of answer derives from the attitudes toward having children and family planning which mitigate against the effective use of contraceptives and tend to produce larger families than are desired or can be provided for by the parents. Thus a man may experience increasing pressure to desert as the size of his family increases, and he may not marry a girl in the first place because she has already had too

---

economic well being, . . . the white population has made greater strides." It notes further that the chance that a person would be living in poverty was three-and-one-half times as great if he were nonwhite than if he were white in 1966—an increase of a half of a per cent over 1959 (pp. 2 and 3).

[5] The conception of familial status advocated by Talcott Parsons and Robert Bales in *Family Socialization and Interaction Process* (New York: The Free Press, 1955), which sees family status as largely or solely determined by status in the larger society, by virtue of the husband-father's occupation, needs qualification, but as a generalized ideal it pervades the project and the ghetto around it. However, in the ghetto a man's familial status may be more significantly determined by other factors (such as his faithfulness and devotion to his children, or his phantom role or "front"), although he can never escape evaluation by the larger society's standards.

[6] Street life is not to be equated with the concept of the "culture of poverty," although it has a style of life that could be called a "culture" in the broadest sense. Oscar Lewis, *La Vida* (New York: Random House, Inc., 1965), estimates that perhaps 10 per cent of the American poor are in the culture of poverty as he defines it. Street life is perhaps but one aspect of the life experienced by the majority of ghetto poor. Only those Jessie Bernard, *Marriage and Family Among Negroes* (Englewood Cliffs, N.J.: Prentice-Hall, Inc., 1966), would label "respectable" shy away from it—and so even they confront it by virtue of their rejection of it.

many children. One child brought to marriage seems not to create any particular problems. Three or four children, born "outside" or as the result of a previous marriage that failed, tend to make a man, already uncertain of his ability to provide and generally resentful of children not his own, think twice before becoming committed in marriage. The conflict in what is considered to be an ideal marriage will be examined first.

Marriage as an Ideal

The people of the project speak about marriage as an ideal in several ways. Young people in their late teens and early twenties see marriage in a way strongly influenced by the street world. A man of twenty says:

> The best kind of marriage is one where you've got an understanding . . . like, you take Jil and I. She knows that I go in for other women, but we just got an understanding that we go out on one another and I don't have to lose interest in women and she doesn't have to lose her interest in men just because we are getting married.

This man is not at present married. What he describes is talked about fairly often in the project. It can be called the "free man, free woman" [7] type of marriage, where both husband and wife are free to pursue outside interests while returning to one another for help and comfort. Such an arrangement attributes great magnanimity to both sexes and defines marriage as a minimal commitment. It follows from the fear of being "put in a trick" or of being used by the other, and is indicative of a basic mistrust of the other—particularly the other sex.

Such a conception of an ideal marriage is advanced even though everyone knows that such relationships are full of trouble. Gerald

[7] This terminology is borrowed from a typology in "Notes" by Lee Rainwater on the problem of "separateness and connectedness" in project families—a problem posed by Robert D. Hess and Gerald Handel in *Family Worlds* (Chicago: University of Chicago Press, 1959). My typology, however, is a modification of his, excluding (among other aspects) this particular type because it was not found in my sample and because it is not as common in the project (I would argue) as the types included in my typology.

Buchanan (eighteen) brings this into focus while explaining why most sexual intercourse in the project occurs during the day.

> You know most of the people around here, their husbands work and they surely don't want to have anything while he's at home. Most of these husbands go berserk. That's the reason you hear about all these killings. . . . He thinks he's a loyal husband and he don't understand how she could do such a thing to him. . . . He probably has a girlfriend too but it just doesn't come out.

In a community with a high percentage of female-headed households and a high percentage of unemployment, the opportunity to "cut out" on a spouse is always present, particularly for the male.

While no dependable data are available for the project as a whole, one has the impression that "cutting out" is very much a part of the married life of persons living in the project.[8] The ideal expressed above as a "free man, free woman" type of relationship, however, is probably characteristic of only a minority of marriages in an early stage of their development. What seems more characteristic of project families is the pattern wherein the woman remains faithful (whether out of principle, concern for her children, or simply because of the fact that she has lost a great deal of her sexual appeal because of her age and her children) and the husband "cuts out." He does this either discreetly or indiscreetly.

Such an ideal does not go unchallenged in the project. Henry Harbison, who has been married over fifty years and who worked until he was seventy-two, supporting his home and raising nine children, remarks:

[8] The attempt to obtain sexual histories by questionnaire techniques during the summer of 1965 resulted in responses felt to be generally accurate in what was reported but lacking in comprehensiveness. Genealogical data collected on the ten families, however, indicate that of the 637 relationships recorded, 18.2 per cent were "visiting" (nonmarital, nonresidential) relationships producing a total of 180 illegitimate children (about 8.8 per cent of the 2,058 persons placed on the genealogies). So also, the percentage of marriages recorded in these genealogies was 51.5 per cent of the total of all relationships. While neither of these figures measures directly the phenomenon of cutting out, they suggest that the frequency is high because the marital bond is so often avoided or broken. On the other hand, death was the greatest "cause" of broken homes, accounting for over 50 per cent of all broken relationships; the majority (60 per cent) of couples still alive lived in complete families. There is also slightly greater evidence of visiting in the genealogies of persons now living in incomplete families (21 per cent versus 15.2 per cent).

> Take a lot of women . . . some got husbands and some got "hubbies." . . . To my way of thinking a husband will care for his family and try and make a home for his wife . . . and your hubbie, he'll just take his family and maybe he'll [cut out] on the weekends. Instead of staying home, he goes out and sets up a date. . . . He may not come in till Sunday or maybe Monday morning.

He recognizes the existence of the promiscuous type of marriage but by word and deed speaks out against it. However, in his conception only the "free man" type is described. What is contrasted is a husband who cares for his family and home and one who does not. The husband as a provider is implied, but what is stressed is his emotional involvement and his faithfulness. On the other hand, the fact that a relationship is entered into lightly does not guarantee—even in the project—that the marriage will not last. One woman of about fifty-five found her fourth husband in the following manner:

> I was living over there [outside the project] and I was out looking around, going around the bars and being seen. One day I was walking down the street and I saw Mr. W. He walks up and says, "Hey there now. I know who you is, just can't call your name. What is your name?"
>
> "Why," I said, "my name is Rosie," and then he said . . .
>
> "Rosie, I'd like to have you for myself. I sure would."

This occurred in 1948. She claims she accepted his proposal immediately and the marriage lasted fourteen years, terminating with his death in 1962. The pattern of bar-hopping to be seen is characteristic of one type of woman used to the ways of the city. This story indicates that a relationship of considerable duration can sometimes, in the context of this community, be initiated quite rapidly with a minimum of fanfare and ceremony—and a minimum of knowledge about each other. This is true in part because a characteristic type of conjugal bond in the project is what Bott has called the segregated conjugal bond where, on the basis of numerous "working understandings," he goes his way and she hers.[9]

[9] Elizabeth Bott, *Family and Social Network* (London: Tavistock Publications, 1957).

A second conception of an ideal marriage stresses the provider role of the husband-father. Mary Perry remarked before her marriage:

> . . . If I can find some boy who's going to give me a home of my own and going to treat me nice . . . take me out sometimes and on a few dates . . . and keep plenty of food in the house . . . and drink . . . and if we have a child, I might want to go out some night . . . and we'd get a baby-sitter to keep the child. . . . If we could agree to all business and make sure everything worked out that way . . . I wouldn't mind getting married myself.

Her conception of marriage, being largely in terms of what her husband could do for her, is in stark contrast to what commonly happens. It is clear also that her conception of married life does not reflect a desire to "settle down." Rather, it stresses going out and enjoying life and letting the baby-sitter take care of the child. It is a statement of wishful thinking only too painfully recognized as largely unattainable.

But the fact that it persists as an ideal makes the comparatively feeble accomplishments of most ghetto husbands as providers all the more intolerable. Young wives just do not understand their husbands' inabilities to effectively compete in the job market. The situation is worsened when a couple moves from the country to the city. There his sharecropper farm pretty well defined his occupational fate and their style of life, and his wife understood this. In the city, however, they see people doing much better than they. This is likely to create a revolution in expectations (particularly on the wife's part) that can have quite negative consequences for their marriage.

One might finally then ask what, in fact, is the value of a *legal* marriage to women like Ethyl Perry and Tilly Hardy.[10] In the case of Ethyl's husband, it has not guaranteed her any income simply because her husband refused to pay and no one has pressed the case hard enough to make him pay child support. In many instances the husband might not be able to pay even if pressed. In Tilly's case

[10] One wonders if church marriages fare better in this context than civil marriages. I think that they would tend to be more stable because the people who would tend to be married in a church in this environment also would tend to be more organized.

her husbands support their children if they can be caught before they spend, but her boyfriend supports her equally as much and does so voluntarily. Betty Re Buchanan insists that she had her reasons for forcing Della and T.J. to marry. She reiterates her concern that grandchildren "have names." She adds that the marriage license gives her power over T.J. to force him to support his children. When asked why she has not used this power in the nearly one year that they have been married, she replies that she does not want to jeopardize the possibility of their making a success of their marriage.

In point of fact, a legal marriage seems of little value in assuring support; nor does it seem, in and of itself, to insure the stability of the conjugal relationship. Many of the women interviewed have gone with their boyfriends longer than they lived with their husbands. It does seem to make remarriage a bit more difficult because of the expense of divorce, but then one wonders how many persons in this setting remarry without bothering to obtain a divorce. Where there is little problem of inheritance and a great amount of "living," there is little pressure to check bigamous relationships—welfare examinations being a notable exception.

The Problem of Unwanted Pregnancy

The matter of early intercourse is not a problem for most families, but pregnancy outside of marriage is. It is perhaps strange that parents do not do a better job of educating their children in the matter of birth control. The Buchanans, for example, are raising their children in the Catholic Church, but even though they make use of the services of the church, they do not consider themselves to be members. The teaching about birth control is not regarded as binding on them. Andrew has read quite extensively on problems connected with poverty and is aware of his own personal problems as a result of a failure to limit his family. "We were eight or nine children out before we even considered doing something about it." After the birth of triplets, Betty Re had her tubes tied. They cannot point to their own success in solving this problem, but they know that it is a real one and that their children would be better off if they had known how to deal with the matter. Yet all they do is tell the children to associate with the right kind of people.

In their daughter Della's case, she did not make love in situations where she was taken by surprise. She knew in advance that T.J. was going to make love to her. Yet, she conceived "outside" when she was sixteen. Part of the reluctance to take advantage of what contraceptives are available may be tied in with a point that is important to Della. She insists, "I didn't really say it was all right for him to make love to me." Had she prepared, she would not be able to use this excuse.

Her brother Gerald has had two "outside kids." He is eighteen. In Gerald's case he contends that condoms are too expensive and detract from his pleasure, and for a while his girl Mary had convinced him that she was using preventatives. Further, both Mary's parents and his own made a definite point at the beginning of his relationship with Mary of determining that "his intentions were honorable." When he was able to convince them that they were, he gained enough access to Mary's apartment that there was no need to make love in situations where one might be hurried or surprised. Mary claims that she did use "jelly" for a time, but that on the night she conceived she had run out. Her second pregnancy was intentional in order to trap Gerald into marrying her.

One might wonder at the wisdom involved in considering that both early sexual relations are natural and that illegitimate children are unnatural and unwanted when one considers the pervasiveness of the failure to use contraceptives. Having said that much folklore is against the use of such devices (the cancer scare is a late addition), and noting further the folk notion that having children is good for a woman's health (if she doesn't have them she's likely to get sick), and finally recognizing that there is an expressed desire to have large families (the latter two give one the impression that they are rationalizations resulting from an inability to control the situation), one is led to speculate more fully on the nature of the risk that is involved in having children out of wedlock.

While the consequences of pregnancy outside of marriage are not as severe as in middle-class society, there are consequences nonetheless. The boyfriend, even if he wanted to support the child, in most instances can offer only token help. The girl's parents are generally pressed for resources and her child, though welcomed, puts a noticeable strain on the family economy. Her chances in the marriage market are restricted. Her parents are inevitably "hurt" because she got pregnant and because she dropped out of high school. Her chances of going on to find a career (a matter of extreme importance when you cannot count on your husband to support you, if and when you find one) are lessened considerably. Pregnancy quite understandably terminates many a girl's career plans.[11] Finally, after marriage, an "outside" child is not completely accepted by his half-siblings. For example, Mary Perry, the outsider, is accused of not being a full sibling when a family feud breaks out. Of course, these consequences are mitigated somewhat by the fact that in many instances the maternal grandmother (or some other relative) "adopts" the child and cares for him even after the girl marries. Illegitimacy as such, then, is not as "serious" as in middle-class society. The birth of a child is an accepted mark of adulthood no matter when the child comes, even though the girl may not care for it herself.

Another positive aspect of pregnancy out of wedlock is that it may be used in catching a husband. To intentionally become pregnant in order to get a husband presupposes the existence of norms that dictate a man's responsibility to care for what he has brought into the world.[12] In the Buchanan family this norm was upheld and reinforced by another that prescribes against "children without fathers." Thus there is an ethic of responsibility that goes beyond the general assertion that when all else fails, "we take care of our own [children], while the white folk give them away."

After marriage the matter of family planning is of concern to project families, but it is rarely effectively utilized. Six women have approached the end of their likely childbearing period. Of these, two had their tubes tied after having borne several more children than

[11] One third of the teenage girls (five out of fifteen) in this age group are married or have children. None has completed high school. Seven out of ten of their mothers also conceived "outside."

[12] Charles C. Willie, *op. cit.*, argues that "the illegitimate child is frequently a by-product of the girl's search for a husband. Viewed in this perspective, out-of-wedlock conception represents not so much a breakdown in family structure, but a broken promise."

desired, and two are unable to bear children because of an operation connected with their last delivery. The matter is thus "existential" for only four mothers who are in their thirties. One of these mothers is also probably sterile because of post-operative difficulties connected with pregnancy though, at the present time, she is not sure. The remaining three feel that they must practice some form of contraception in order to avoid pregnancy. Since two of these have miscarried recently, although not desiring more children, it seems reasonable to assume that they are not very effective practitioners.[13]

Matters of sex are not discussed in project families. A wife is supposed to accommodate her husband and the matter of the wife's satisfaction is not often considered. One wife claims:

> I know what he can do and when he just gets up there and satisfies himself and I'm left hung up in the air and everything, then I'm ready to kill him. My first thought was to run out in the streets to get satisfaction, but I don't want that.

Another wife has still another reason for her dissatisfaction with marital sex:

> Something happened to my husband. My husband don't get his kicks. As I tell him, I can't let him ride me for two or three hours because I have feelings. And well that makes him angry but that's nothing to get angry over because after all, I am a human being. I'm going to try to please him true enough, but after all, if it's going to mean at least two or three hours, I just can't do that.

Because marital sex is perceived as largely a matter of satisfying the male, his wishes with regard to the use of condoms are respected. Generally he does not like them because they interfere with his pleasure. The devices used are commonly not the most effective available

[13] Lee Rainwater, *And the Poor Get Children* (Chicago: Quadrangle Books, 1960), describes the working-class's problems as largely those of ineffective use of contraceptives, not so much because the technique utilized was not the most effective but because whatever technique is utilized, is utilized ineffectively. A major finding of this study was that these people had a lot of information about contraceptives, and in fact practiced the use of a wide variety of techniques to prevent contraception—but did not practice effectively.

and are quite often used only sporadically. As a result, most couples confess to having more children than they desire.[14]

These ten women have borne sixty-five children by their husbands.

Problems in Earning a Living[15]

Clearly the most pressing problem facing project families is that of earning a living. Although the majority of project families are headed by females, employment of some sort accounts for at least part of the family income in 61 per cent of the households. It is the principal source of income in 45 per cent of the total households, and in 76 per cent of the households headed by males.[16] Various forms of welfare assistance make up the remainder of these families' incomes. Contrary to popular opinion, welfare is sought as a last resort and is quite insufficient to sustain a family above the poverty level.[17] Sixty-five per cent of the households have incomes less than the Social Security Administration's poverty level. Only 19 per cent of the households headed by females exceed this level.[18]

In the case of the ten families under close scrutiny, however, wages are the principal source of income in only two cases, although they contribute to the family's income in five other instances. The various sources of this income are given in Table I in Chapter 1. Only one of

[14] This is certainly true of the ten mothers and, although the results of our sample survey have not been tabulated in this area, I would surmise on the basis of my impression of about forty families whom I interviewed personally that it would be true here also.

[15] Data in this section depend in part upon information collected by the Intervention Staff. The author wishes to thank Dr. Alvin W. Gouldner and his assistants, Dr. William Yancey, Martin Liebowitz, and Joyce Ladner, for making the mimeographed report "Intervention Research: The Case of Unemployment" available.

[16] These statements are based on a sample survey conducted in the summer of 1965 (N = 162) and interpreted by Jerome Stromberg, "A Preliminary Report on Housing and Community Experiences of (Project) Residents" (St. Louis: The Social Science Institute of Washington University, 1966), p. 33.

[17] In a nation that fancies itself to be hopelessly becoming a welfare state only about one fifth of the poor were covered by welfare in 1963 (considering the poverty population to be 35 million persons and the number of persons on welfare to be a little over 7.5 million). *Health, Education and Welfare Indicators* (December 1963), p. 40.

[18] Stromberg, *op. cit.*, p. 34.

these families had an income that could be considered above the poverty level in 1966.[19] These figures, however, provide only a rough indication of the economic constraints placed upon these families.[20]

The reasons why earning a living is such a difficult problem are many and complexly intertwined. Consider first the matter of education, often thought to be the key to success in America and the basis for any sound policy that hopes to erradicate poverty.

Education

Most of the fifteen parents in these ten families came to the city from the rural South. In the country they had less need for an education, and most of them did not seek nor were encouraged to obtain one. The average number of years of formal schooling of the five

[19] A comparison of family incomes in 1965 and the corresponding poverty level figures follows:

Family Income—1965		Number of Persons	Poverty Level Income—1965*
Buchanans	$6,720	18	$7,910 (family of 11)
Pattersons	6,072	10	7,500#
Washingtons	4,370†	8	6,200#
Fraziers	4,896	11	7,910
Billits	2,148	5	3,930
Perrys	3,144	4	3,320
Parvins	2,148	7	5,400
Wards	4,824	5	3,930
Browns	3,888	8	6,200#
Handys	6,540	11	7,910#

* Based on the computations of Mollie Orshansky, *Social Security Bulletin*, XXVIII, "Counting the Poor: Another Look at the Poverty Profile" (Washington, D. C.: The U. S. Government Printing Office, January 1965), Table E. Roughly these figures are three times the computed cost of a minimum but adequate diet.

These figures are based on extrapolation from Orshansky's figures.

† Figure does not include unknown income from gambling.

[20] Because such factors are not able to reflect all sources of income (particularly illegitimate), because the composition of the household varies so much throughout the year, and because most sources of income other than welfare are quite undependable, the figures given are probably optimistic rather than conservative. As Table I indicates, when there is a family income for 1965 in the Housing Authority files, it is usually lower than the figure utilized here.

fathers, therefore, is 4.4 years; their wives as well as those women heading households have an average of 7.8 years of schooling. One mother, Alliena Billit, attended college one year.[21]

On the average, their children are 1.5 years behind in school and over two years behind when they graduate from grade school. This means that boys and girls in the project ordinarily get out of grade school when they are over fifteen. Only the Billit children are not behind. In the rest of the families from 60 to 89 per cent of the children are below their grade level. Although I.Q. is a poor measure of intelligence, it does provide some indication of the extent to which a child is handicapped in the school system. Of the eighty-five project children in school, only five have I.Q.'s between 100 and 125, the average I.Q. being in the 80's.[22] Finally, in the case of twenty-seven children who had their I.Q.'s measured two or more times, twenty scored *lower* the second time.[23] Education, *as they experience it,* is a handicap, not a help.

It is not surprising that during 1963–1967 only three children graduated from high school, one of these by means of an equivalency examination. One boy, T. J. Patterson, went to work on an assembly line for a few months before he quit and joined the unemployed. Luemer Wards continued to work as a sales clerk in a local department store. Education does not mean upward mobility for project residents in the same way that it does for the middle class.[24] They

[21] Stromberg, *op. cit.,* p. 20, indicates that this is slightly below the level of education common to project parents, where the men have an average of 9.6 years of schooling and the women 8.7 (N = 156).

[22] These data are computed from records of the city school system and are given fuller treatment in David A. Schulz, "Variations in Complete and Incomplete Families of the Negro Lower-Class" (unpublished Doctoral dissertation, Washington University, 1968), Appendix C and Tables XIV and XV.

[23] This pattern of I.Q. deterioration seems characteristic of ghetto schools. Kenneth Clark charted a similar pattern for Harlem schools in his study, *Youth in the Ghetto* (New York: Harlem Youth Opportunities Unlimited, Inc., 1964), pp. 178 ff.

[24] Indeed, according to the mid-decade census, the income for Negroes who have completed some or all of their college is a lesser proportion of the comparable white income than incomes of Negro grade school graduates compared to their white counterparts. In other words, black Americans *earn* comparatively less for *learning* more. United States Department of Labor, "Social and Economic Conditions of Negroes in the United States," *Current Population Reports* (Washington, D.C.: United States Government Printing Office, October 1967), p. 21.

rarely see its rewards and can, if they desire, earn more illegitimately without it than they can earn legitimately with an education.

Nevertheless parents speak often of the desirability of their children getting an education. Ethyl Perry commented about her daughter Mary's school work in 1964:

> The best thing I want her to do is to finish school and then if she's able to go to college, I can help her and she can work. . . . Sometimes she say, "I don't know why we have to go to school. I don't feel like it." I used to say, "You go on and see the nurse, and the nurse will send you home if you shouldn't be there!" . . . I guess she just want to be playin'. . . . I make her go anyway.

None of Ethyl's children has completed high school and none seems likely to, even though many express a desire to do so. James joined the Army before graduating, Mary got pregnant and has not returned. The younger children are not enthusiastic students. The pattern is common. Most families have several children at home during the school week because they are "sick" or do not have shoes or proper dress. Sometimes these excuses seem valid; often they do not.

School is a problem for project children from the very start. Their poverty prevents them from having such basic prerequisites as sufficient food during the month and adequate privacy for sleep and study. Their environment does not provide enough interesting and varied objects for young hands and minds to explore. The level of conversation in the home is generally low and of poor quality.

As a rule the parents do not encourage their children by praising them for good grades and are not able to help them with their homework since their own education is generally poor. They are normally concerned that their children attend school but will accept, as part of their lenient stance toward children, almost any excuse that will enable them not to go. As a result, education is achieved by and large in spite of the home environment and not because of its assistance.[25] When one couples this with the lower rewards available to

[25] A detailed account of the problems these project families present for the educational system can be found in William Moore, "A Portrait: The Culturally Disadvantaged Pre-School Negro Child" (unpublished Doctoral dissertation, St. Louis University, 1964). Despite the home difficulties, however, Kenneth Clark dis-

those who do manage to get an education in ghetto schools, it is not difficult to see why education is such a problem for ghetto children. These children, in all probability, will have a better education than their parents, but it will not be good enough to get them the jobs they want. This is true both because the level of education required to hold a good job is increasing and because racial discrimination still prevents the Negro from having an equal opportunity.

Job Discrimination

Parents and children alike are uncertain about the effects of racial discrimination because they are aware that they come to the job with a minimum of qualifications and because the excuses given by employers often seem plausible. They are not prone to complain about racial discrimination in employment. Yet it cannot be doubted that such discrimination is a major factor for the Negro in America.[26] Project residents experience it also. Some, indeed, do complain. Mary Perry (eighteen) recalls her early employment "down home":

> I worked in a store once when I was in Birmingham, Alabama. I was in a confectionary. I was the checker behind the counter. . . . I was making $25.00 a week and I was surprised at that too. . . . Of course I was working for my own colored people. [That's why] I made that much. 'Cause down South, you know, colored kids don't make that much money a week.

Also in the city "the man" has the edge. He owns most of the ghetto stores in the project area. Sam (seventeen) reflects "They [the white folk] almost own most of the stores. Not all of them, but most of them." Even if you can get a job in these stores, wages are low.

Sometimes the malpractice cannot directly be attributed to race but because such practices are common among the poor, they affect the Negro proportionately more than the white. Thus Lester Frazier re-

---

covered that the most significant predictor of a ghetto child's success in the Harlem schools was the attitude of the school administrators. Where much was expected, more was accomplished.

[26] As has been noted, holding education constant increases the poverty gap between white and non-white and, although improvements have been made for the population as a whole, the non-white portion has not shared equally.

calls his experience working for a filling station manager in the city:

> I worked there near about three years. . . . Some weeks I would make $55.00 and I'd bring home about $49.00 after they took out. I wasn't in the union. . . . They told me I had to work thirty days before getting in the union. When thirty days come, he laid me off for about two or three days. That was to keep from putting me in the union. . . . When he hire me back I'd go ahead on back to work. I thought, "Maybe he's going to put me in the union this week."

Lester never directly accused the white station manager of discrimination, but all of his past experience down South led him to be quite suspicious of such treatment. In any event, such treatment effectively keeps him in his place up North as well.

Finally, Mr. Jackson, a construction worker who normally works in a lumber yard but who finds himself unemployed every winter, does not hesitate to describe the discrimination he sees. He puts it this way:

> Well my wife, she never breathes down my collar about unemployment. She have the understanding what we goes up against and how hard it is for a colored man to get a job when he gets out and the whole world understand that. There are no "oohs and aahs" about it. You know what I mean. There's no use in asking questions when you know there's facts there.[27]

Many wives, however, do not stop complaining about their husband's unemployment and, like Alliena Billit, they will not work for their husband when he is not working.

Skills Acquired on the Job

Not only do men in the project come seeking a job with poor records of formal education and fearful of prejudice and discrimination, they also come with few skills that they have learned on their previous job. It is a part of the cumulation of disadvantages that all

[27] These quotes are from an intervention study conducted by the Intervention Staff, "Intervention Research: The Case of Unemployment" (internal working paper).

poor people face, but the Negro seems lower down the occupational scale generally.

In the project in 1965, 40 per cent of the men were "unskilled and custodial workers in private firms" and 20 per cent were unemployed or on welfare. Only 24 per cent were semiskilled or skilled workers and 2 per cent were clerical.[28] The kinds of jobs they could look forward to included janitorial work, night watchman, non-union truck driver, dishwasher, waiter, lumberyard worker, furnace stoker in a foundry, assembly line operator, elevator operator, cab driver, porter, and unskilled construction work (ditch digger, hod carrier, etc.). They also could go into business on their own, either to supplement welfare payments if they were disabled or to supplement their wives' earnings as domestics. They might operate a moving business with an old dilapidated truck or the family car. Some repair appliances, start lawn care businesses, or work for the various anti-poverty programs (organizing project residents or providing services for their families).[29] In the summer, the young may apply for training in the job corps. Only two youths tried such a route. One father talked about being retrained as a cook.

In very few of these jobs could one acquire a skill that has some market value. The TV, small appliance, or automobile repair businesses are often undertaken without any previous training. Customers are frequently disappointed with the results but, because "the price was right," they continue to be patient. The amount of money earned in illegal activities is unknown, although most men admit to gambling and some to promoting gambling activities such as policy.

The mothers find most of their employment in part-time activities such as baby-sitting and day work. A few work for hotels as maids, for local stores as sales girls, for such organizations as the Urban League, for the school system in the fall and winter, or as nurses' aides. Others find ways to supplement their income by sewing, ironing, or quilting in their homes. The teenage girls look forward to jobs as nurses or secretaries, but they know few people in their project who are employed in these jobs. The mother's wage is the main source of family

[28] Stromberg, *op. cit.*, p. 29.

[29] This list of occupations is derived from the data collected on the persons over sixteen in the ten families who provide the basic qualitative data for this study plus two additional families who are less well known.

income in only one instance, however. In most cases the women are "on welfare" or supplement their husband's income by means of part-time employment.

Attitude Toward a Job

The awareness of the problems faced by a black man seeking work in America has resulted in varying attitudes toward obtaining a job. The most startling difference in attitudes is between the young and the old men. The men over thirty-five in the project have a distinctively different attitude toward work than the younger men. Lester Frazier gives a characteristic response of the older men:

> I had started working for a guy for $20.00 a week hauling cardboard. I had to do something. . . . That's the only way I could get anything to buy something to eat, so I had to take that job for $20.00 a week [about 1961] until I could do better. . . . I said making *some* money is better than making none.

Henry Harbison, now retired at seventy-three, makes the contrast clear:

> I just kind of fell into that job. . . . I took it figuring until I got something better a little later. [It payed] six bits an hour [about 1949]. I figures a little job is better than none. . . . Some fellow figures that he can't get good wages he won't work, but I always figure that a little job's better than none.

So he took the job in a furniture warehouse for seventy-five cents an hour, and a few weeks later he found another one in a produce department that paid more and was more dependable.

The younger men, characteristically, will not work for the sake of working until they find a better job. For them "a little job" is *not* "better than none." They will wait around, often becoming discouraged or infuriated at not finding the job they want, or they will work sporadically at a job they do not like, waiting until they get one or two weeks' pay before quitting. In such a situation, they fall back on their mothers [as in the case of Gerald Buchanan (eighteen) or T. J. Patterson (nineteen)], or if they are older they try living off women—"living sweet"—for a while, or they earn money illegally, or simply do nothing and "take what comes."

A part of their problem undoubtedly is the frustration incurred from expanding expectations concerning what is desirable and exaggerated concepts of what a high school education can do for a person in the 1960's. Feeling themselves barred from the apprenticeship programs in the more interesting or lucrative jobs (electrician, bricklayer, painter, etc.) and unable to afford—even if they were willing to take—further education, they perceive themselves effectively cut off from the American dream.

Looking for a Job

Despite what, from a middle-class perspective, might be perceived as a foolish, stubborn, or lazy attitude toward work, the young men are in fact faced with great difficulties in finding jobs, given who they are. Jerry Jackson inquired about a job advertised in a newspaper. "They asked if I was white or colored. When I told them I was colored, they said the job was filled." During his off season Jerry was encouraged to seek employment. It was estimated that he covered 250 miles, spent nine dollars on gas and thirty-five hours in the field, and made inquiry at 131 different locations during the course of a single week. At only one of these did he feel that he had a very good possibility of finding a job.[30] He explained:

> Things are awfully slow now. Well it's winter. You know this is the season when they start counting and getting everything ready to start again. Now you see I worked in these kinds of plants before. And this is the time when they take inventory for the next year getting ready to put it on sale.

In the city, construction work slows down in the winter and most industry connected with it (such as the lumber yard where Mr. Jackson works during the spring and summer) is also slowed down. His impression of the work year is thus strongly influenced by his experience in cyclical employment in the construction business. Further-

[30] A complete account of the experience of Mr. Jackson's search for a job is presented in "Intervention Research: The Case of Unemployment."

more, his lumber yard job, which is not able to employ him the entire year, teaches him no skills that can help him get another job. He thinks of himself as a construction worker and accordingly seeks jobs largely in this area. He is thus assured of a minimal job, but this in turn makes it difficult for him to seek a better job.

Once he worked for a car wash in the winter. He quit because of low wages and the miserable working conditions. The precipitating event was his boss's request that he wash cars in sub-zero weather, but there were other incidents as well:

> I would rather starve, lie down and eat dirt than work for a man who cussed me. He wanted to check my time. Well, I know how to check my time. *He didn't think I was a man. And didn't treat me like a man.* Yeah, I walked off that job.

Clearly, it is important for Jerry Jackson not only to earn money but also to be treated decently and to be thought of as a responsible man. When he did not receive this treatment, he quit.

When not specifically encouraged to seek jobs, men in the project ordinarily rely on friends who are employed to keep them informed of employment opportunities. Want ads are frequently utilized and followed through with phone calls or bus trips. The Jewish Employment Agency has a good reputation with some project residents because they feel that this agency is now working hard to find jobs for lower-class Negro men. Local church organizations are sometimes contacted. The one agency that is almost always neglected is the state employment agency, because project residents do not feel that this agency has other than menial jobs available. Further, they do not understand the referral system that is frequently employed. To wait several hours in the agency's impersonal waiting rooms, is, therefore, considered a waste of good time. Jerry Jackson, for example, did not seek help from this agency until he was paid to do so, and then his experience confirmed his preconceptions.

The net result is that project families have very inadequate incomes that fluctuate from year to year and throughout the year as seasonal employment gives way to unemployment compensation, and even that is finally exhausted. Unskilled, poorly paid jobs, even if full-time, do not provide economic security. Indeed, economic security is something the project families rarely, if ever, experience.

Selected Trajectories of Family Income

Job Histories

Henry Harbison came to the city in 1949. He and his wife had both picked cotton in the fields of the South and had come North seeking better times. Being of the old school, Henry had but three jobs during his employment in the city. He took his first job so that he could put some food on the table. It was as a freight handler in a furniture warehouse. After a few weeks he worked for a local food chain:

> I worked as a janitor and I unloaded trailers and I helped unload the freight, lifted 100 pound sacks of potatoes. . . . I've done my share of hard work in my life. . . . Now you take those ice box cars. You've got to shovel 2,000 pounds of ice before you can even move the stuff inside of them and you put rubber gloves on to keep your hands from getting wet, but that don't keep them from freezing. I worked in those cars sometimes when it was zero outside and lifted those bales and piled them on top of one another.

Although completely unskilled, he sought work as a machine operator with a small manufacturing firm in the early 1950s:

> I was a machine operator and the foreman, he told me, "Now you turn the switch here and it turns the machine on and you adjust this dial and that works up and down a little bit and you adjust these things, makes it go a little better," and then he turned around and left. I worked the machine and a couple of days later he came around and asked me to work another machine and so he showed me how to adjust this and turn that knob and start this thing and I started her up. He told the boss, he said, "There's a man who learns real quick."

Several of the men show great pride in their ability to learn such semiskilled jobs. Lester Frazier, however, feels that he was able to learn more in the South because "the man" down there wouldn't pay you, but at least he let him do a lot of things (like drive a tractor) which white men up North are unwilling to let him do.

Henry's job with this small manufacturer lasted over ten years. When he retired at the age of seventy-two, he was earning $1.99 an hour. He was not employed full-time during his last years with his company, and so he earned only $2,729 in 1963, the year before his retirement. His wife's sister received about $444 in disability that year, giving his family (three persons) an income of $3,172. Upon his retirement, he received $18.75 per month from his company plus his old age assistance and social security.

Harry Harrison has lived in the city all his life. He began his job career not in the cotton fields but in the steel foundries. He was a "heat boy" at fifteen. The job consisted mainly in tending the furnaces so that they would maintain the proper temperature. He worked his way up in the foundry and after about ten years was doing some riveting and working as a "chain man." When the furnaces were automated, he was laid off. He continued his interest in riveting at a company manufacturing railroad cars:

> I saw that it was interesting work and something that not everyone could do. See, in riveting there are about seven kinds of rivets. You got to memorize which one to use where. You put them on a shovel and stick that shovel in the furnace. If you get them too hot they run together and melt. If you get it too cold they won't squeeze. The thing to do is you got to get them just right, so you have to watch and adjust it. I use the tongs and then the rivet man he takes them and puts them in the holes and squeezes them tight.

Having said that he was a man interested in riveting, it turned out that in fact he was the man who heated the rivets. Another man exercised the skill in selection and in insertion. While working for the car company, he was injured seriously and was put on complete and total disability in 1961. He now receives $65.00 a month for this disability, works part-time at some repair work, moves people with his car, and claims that he is looking for another job. The job he is seeking requires skill. The welfare office once thought it could find him some work:

> They asked me if I would be interested in getting trained to do a new job. I said I would, and they sent me to a whole slew of doctors. I believe I went to see three downtown and then they told me I got to go to one up on Brand Avenue. If these doctors say it is okay, then they going to tell me. They asked me to put down what I was interested in doing, and they going to get me a job. So I put down TV repair, and electronics, and then if I couldn't get that I put down carpentry and plumbing. I made that table over there. . . .

Even though Harry considers himself talented and has been able to earn some money repairing various things around his home, he can see where some people are not so fortunate. He sees automation as providing jobs for some, but putting many others out of work:

> I think they ought to make jobs for them, because if a man can't get a job, he can't support his family. . . . A man can't help it if he is born without talent. I don't think he should have to sit around, be turned loose. . . . If a man can work I think he would rather work. Now you take me, for instance, I am going to try and get that job so I can get off this piddling amount of money that I am getting now and maybe make some real money.

The income for the Harrison family in 1963 included $840 a year in disability payments and $2,424 for ADC, giving a total of $3,264 for a family of ten. This amount was supplemented by an unknown amount of income from Harry's odd jobs and his wife's baby-sitting.

Both Henry Harbison and Harry Harrison are atypical since they had only a few jobs before retirement. The case of Arthur Washington in more typical. In Table IV one sees an impersonal history of a marriage. While it is quite clear that much is left unsaid by these figures, a great deal is told. The Washingtons have lived together for twenty-six years. During this time, Arthur has gone from the major wage earner to one that supplements his wife's income by whatever means he can find. His income from illegitimate sources is not included.

Three factors vital to Arthur's role as a provider seem to have been largely beyond his control. His family increased on the average of one child every two years until he had eleven children and his wife had

Table IV BRIEF ECONOMIC HISTORY OF A SINGLE FAMILY*

Year	Number of Children	Rent	Annual Income	Other Comments
1943	4	$33.50	$2,500	Arthur works on assembly line; wife unemployed.
1947	6	35.00	2,595	
1949	8	39.00	3,439	
1950	8	35.00	2,560	
1956	11	69.00	4,317	July—Son, 16, held at children's building suspected of minor theft. August—Housing Authority submits request for rent in arrears to be paid not later than September 10th.
1957	11	49.00	2,385	Income of husband from major job.
			300	Income of husband from cab job.
			600	U.C.B.
			978	Wife's job as maid in hotel.
			4,263	
				Rent in arrears in the amount of $369.00.
1958	11	33.00	2,503	Income from husband's major job.
		73.00	1,040	Cab company.
		65.00	976	Wife's job.
		34.00	507	U.C.B.
			5,026	
				Husband complains about rent increase. Finally rent is reduced to the $34.00/mo. "hardship" plan.
1959	11	78.00	5,188	Income in approximate distribution as above. Son, 19, robbed a man of $27.00 saying, "I should have killed you when I robbed you."—Report clipped from the local paper. Son, 9, held for breaking a car window. Son, 19, moves out.
1960	11		6,259	Daughter given violation for "loitering," son for "gambling."
1961	11	94.00	6,383	Husband laid off after nineteen years "until further notice."
1963	11	43.00	5,955	Husband has no reported income, wife has two jobs.
1965	8		4,370	Wife's wages plus husband's odd jobs.

* Source—City Housing Authority Files

her tubes tied. During this time his income did not even double, so that in 1956 he was far behind in his rent (over $300) and his wife was forced to go to work. His family, though large, had presented the Housing Authority with few problems prior to 1957, but after his wife went to work and he took a second job, his children "got out of hand" and the record of their violations increased. Only a few are recorded here to indicate the nature of the offenses.[31] When he was dismissed from his major job after nineteen years (another victim of automation), he was unable to find full-time employment though he has often sought it. It is, as we have seen, very difficult for an unskilled or semiskilled man of forty-seven to find work. Hauling jobs and gambling now supplement his wife's income. Seven of the boys have records and one is "on the lam." Nevertheless, the family holds together, and Arthur continues to do the best he can by his children. Had his income increased with his family or had he been able to control his family size, things might have been quite different for his children.

Arthur retains status in his family even though he is only engaged part-time in a legitimate job because his wife knows what he is up against and is willing to tolerate his deviance. Arthur does not make an issue out of his outside activities. His sons have followed his example, having become convinced that an illegal income is the only income that a ghetto youth can expect to earn unless he wants to work for nothing—or depend on welfare.

Welfare

A person goes on welfare when there is nothing else to do. Dorothy Brown went on welfare when she came to the city without relatives and could not find a job. In 1964, she asked to be taken off the welfare rolls, because she felt that she could earn more on her own. All three men receiving disability checks claim that they would rather work because they receive such a "piddling amount" and their wives do not understand their disability. Even with their disability checks and their wives' ADC checks, their families are below the poverty level. Welfare is not intended to provide support that might destroy incentive to work—*even if such incentive is pointless in disabled men.*

The women heading families who are on ADC find, like Ethyl, that the degrading process of labeling has been carried quite far. They are disreputable and perceive that they are thought of as wanting to rear illegitimate children so as to receive additional income. The form that

[31] In addition to numerous Housing Authority violations, the Washington children were arrested fifty times over the ten-year period, 1955–1965, on charges ranging from assault with the intent to kill to petty theft.

they must sign for the Housing Authority promising not to have any more illegitimate children convinces them of this. The system, in other words, does not distinguish between a child that might represent a broken promise (to a woman seeking a good man) and one that was the result of uncontrolled passion or a desire to live off the state.

Nevertheless, eight of the ten families are on some form of welfare and see no real way of getting off. They endure the labeling and the violations of their privacy because it is better than nothing—and often better than they can earn legitimately.

SUMMARY

Marriage, therefore, as a lifelong monogamous union implying exclusive sexual rights is a very difficult objective to realize. In the project the majority of the families are headed by women.[32] Most of these are separated or divorced from their husbands. Many depend in varying degrees upon less formalized relationships with men for income supplement and emotional satisfaction. This high percentage of broken families is not characteristic of the Negro lower-class as a whole, and yet the problems of these families are particularly acute since most of them are poor.[33]

Faced with restrictions upon horizontal and vertical mobility and conspicuous by virtue of skin color, project families have adapted to their environment as best they can. Street culture, under the influence of young male attitudes, advocates a relationship where marriage is a minimum commitment or nonexistent and encourages the male to "live sweet" off his woman. When a man's status depends so much, as it does in our country, upon his capacity to provide for his family,

[32] Myron J. Lefcowitz, "Poverty and Negro-White Family Structure" (Washington, D.C.: Agenda Paper for White House Planning Session on Race, November 1965), estimates on the basis of 1960 census data that 33 per cent of non-white families earning under $3,000 a year were headed by females.

[33] The report "The Extent of Poverty in the United States: 1959–1960" indicates a decrease in the incidence of poverty among non-white families headed by females over the period 1959–1966 from 71.4 per cent to 60.2 per cent. And yet, when family size is taken into account, the percentage of such families in poverty increases to 83.9 per cent for a family with seven or more children in 1966.

such arrangements receive support in the ghetto when the most desirable role is perceived as impossible to obtain.

For the majority of men who do finally legally marry and attempt to settle down, there are great problems in planning a family and earning a living which tend to make them desert. Torn between validating masculine virility and controlling the size of their family, and finding themselves severely handicapped in the job market, many men leave or turn to illegitimate means of earning a living. The income these families receive is thus quite variable. The only really dependable aspects of their financial situation are the increasing cost of living and their decreasing capacity to earn. They "grow old" at forty-seven, and what skills they might have acquired become rapidly obsolete.

With such pressures upon marriage, it is amazing that so many non-white marriages last as long as they do and that the majority of families at any given time in the Negro lower-class are complete. In the ghetto, intimacy and security are found and maintained with much effort and at great risk.

Chapter 6

Summary and Conclusions

In a study attempting to describe something of the complex variation that is found even in a small number of lower-class Negro families, it is difficult to formulate simple conclusions. For every generalization, qualifications can be cited. And yet not to generalize somehow aborts the effort to understand. The interpretation of the dynamics of socialization in project families that follows is undoubtedly a simplification, but less of one than is commonly employed in the sociological literature. Its purpose, in congruence with that of the study as a whole, is to be suggestive. Its application to the entire Negro lower class must depend upon further research.

Parental Ambivalence over Children

The basic mistrust in interpersonal relationships characteristic of lower-class Negro life grows out of a long history of perceived exploitation at the hands of others—particularly those others who are of the opposite sex. Both sexes are well instructed, but the art of manipulation seems best manifested in the pimp, the man who lives off his woman and uses her money to take other women out, thus demonstrating that he doesn't "give a damn" about his benefactress. This mistrust is built into the socialization process very early in a child's life.

Contrary to what one might assume from the evidence of large families and husky smiling women, it is not uncommon for project women to feel themselves "overrun with children." Their tendency to feel this way varies with their birth order. Those born first and consequently forced early to assume the responsibility of raising "her" (i.e., their mother's) children feel the strongest resentment. At nine they were caring for her babies, feeding them and changing their diapers. At thirteen they were "given the children" as their major responsibility. They express a deep-seated anger and resentment against these children, who deprived them of their girlhood, and a strong ambivalence over their own children, who come along later in life and restrict the freedom of their womanhood. They give evidence of experiencing both an intense feeling of guilt over this hatred and a strong desire to identify with their daughters, in an attempt to regain their girlhood vicariously.

This ever-present guilt causes some lower-class mothers to seek compensation in indulging their children and letting them have their way. But the hatred is not thereby dissipated. It remains always in the background and sometimes—particularly in the case of first-born daughters who have become mothers—it breaks through their apparently easygoing and indulgent natures in uncontrollable anger. This anger is so close to the surface in the case of some mothers (e.g., Dorothy Brown and Alliena Billit) that they are afraid to discipline their children for fear that they will go too far and seriously hurt them. Thus the basic mistrust is further reinforced in the socialization process, as children sense, but cannot always define, the nature of their mother's conflict. The boy child feels this most since he offers no compensation by way of identification for his mother, yet demands the same care.

Children quickly learn from their father also that they are not an unmixed blessing. In the city, large families are liabilities, particularly when the father is uncertain of his ability to provide for them. Caught in the pinch between desiring children to validate his masculinity, and experiencing repeated failure in his attempt to provide, the father often deserts. Three of those husband-fathers now living with their wives have done so for periods of time ranging from a few weeks to two years. Before they leave they are likely to exclaim, as did Edward Patterson, "There are just too many kids in this house." Children thus often learn that they are responsible for forcing their father to leave, although they can do nothing about it.

This is not intended to imply that project parents do not love their children, or that they raise children incapable of love. It is intended to say that they raise children who must love in spite of this basic mistrust of interpersonal relationships.

Agonistic Sexual Identities

In the ghetto, the sexes are pitted against each other from an early age. The girl experiences her socialization into an adult sexual role by closely identifying with her mother in the context of the home. This process is less likely to be interrupted and is internally much more consistent than the process by which a boy becomes a man. He must assume his masculine identity under the tutelage of his peers, which requires a "totalistic rearrangement of images" wherein the mother, who was once perceived as the source of all virtue, love, and dependability, must now be seen as a member of the opposite sex who is not to be trusted and indeed who is someone to be "put in a trick."

While the mother governs her daughter's coming up almost consistently from the time she is a baby until the time she marries, a father's influence over his son's development comes about much later than would be the case in white middle-class society. The son finds his father as a teenager. He must break away from his mother largely on his own, by means such as playing the dozens or affirming his masculine identity in the gang. After he has done this, his father then becomes a more acceptable person and thus can influence his future development more effectively. However, because the father was not psychologically "there" when he was needed in the crucial period of breaking away from the mother (even if he were in the home), his dependability remains always suspect, and the young boy, who sees his father as a role model, has great difficulty achieving a sense of his own competence and dependability. He carries a certain negative self-evaluation throughout life as a result. This evaluation encourages his tendency to maintain an apparently competent front and makes him strive to not "lose his cool" in any situation.

The socialization of a boy is further complicated by the fact that his father is less competent as a role model for effective adaptation to modern urban life than his mother is for his sister. Coming from the farms of the South, his father's skills are useless in the city and the task of acquiring appropriate skills is very difficult. Even the masculine chores around the house are no longer needed. Useless around the house and a failure on the job, the father is only instrumentally valuable to the son to the extent that he can train him in the ways of the streets.

In order to become a man in the ghetto, therefore, a boy must earn a "rep" by demonstrating his ability in conquest; for he is not able, within the context of the ghetto family, to obtain and sustain an identity as a respectable family man and a competent provider.

Significantly, men do not call each other "boy" unless they are intent upon insult. "Boy" harks back to the subordinate position under "the man" down South. "Boy" thus has odious racial overtones which remind the project youth that he must become a man in spite of, but constantly in the face of, Whitey. Thus men of forty-five and fifty in the ghetto have experienced the city in a much different way from their wives, whose domestic world has changed relatively little since they were nine.

The girl, for her part, witnesses the exploitation of women by men from the time she is aware of her father's "cutting out" or learns from a pregnant friend where babies come from. She also learns how to jive, how to unmask a weak program (weak line), and how to obtain information (sometimes experience) on sexual matters from her peers, siblings, and mother. Thus she does not enter the sexual arena defenseless. She is, however, suspicious, even when daring to become a player herself and have several men "up tight." A girl knows that a man may not be seeking her for her own sake, but rather for the benefits she can provide, but at the same time she wants to provide these benefits in the context of a stable home to a man who cares for her and her children. Not finding many men who can be depended upon and having already experienced "doing it" as something "natural," she is quite likely to be victimized in seeking a lasting relationship and forced to bear children earlier and in greater number than she expected.

In her early teens a girl must make a choice between pregnancy or a "career." It is put thus bluntly because contraceptive techniques have as yet done little to change the consequence of the "natural" sexuality of ghetto life, and a girl is still likely to become pregnant before she marries. She must either attempt to "please" her boyfriend by "doing it" for him or try to reach some understanding with him that will restrain his interests at least until she gets out of high school.

This decision to please seems to be made by the majority of the girls in the project. The contrary course is very difficult. The choice of a career means not only that one risks offending the boys, but also that one cuts herself off from a central mode of solidifying her relationships with other girls (talking about their love affairs). Further, it defers at least one means of certifying that she has entered womanhood (becoming pregnant). The pressure to defer is lessened further for some girls by the fact that at the age of fourteen they do not know where babies come from and have not the faintest idea of the real consequences of their "doing it." To become pregnant in her mid-teens generally means that a girl will not finish high school and thus will normally not go on to her career as a typist, secretary, or nurse. She has thus been shunted into domestic work before she has fully become aware of the alternatives that might otherwise have been open to her.

Ghetto women are suspicious of masculine advances and strongly conscious of their own femininity. The bond of solidarity they share with all other Negro women is summed up in the use of the one word "girl." Commonly a woman is called "girl" all of her life. A girl is youthful, sexually seductive, and "hip" to the fact that "love is a common word." She is no one's "woman" and is proud of her independence and ability to "go for herself," if necessary without a man. If she has suffered an early pregnancy, she is wiser for her mistakes and remains —symbolically at least—undefiled.

In order to enable a person to overcome the fear of thus being exploited, there is the characteristic lower-class emphasis upon concretizing relationships. A person must constantly demonstrate that he is concerned about his partner. Often this is done by calling many times each day, by stopping by and providing a detailed account of one's activities to the person being wooed, and by many small gifts or regular contributions of cash. Love is indeed a common word, and is meaningless in the ghetto unless it is concretely demonstrated.

Marriage as a lifelong commitment to one woman is exceedingly difficult to realize in the project. The basic mistrust of the opposite sex and the fear of exploitation, the perceived restrictions on mobility, and the handicaps encountered in earning a living made it difficult to contemplate marriage in the first place, and the pressure of increasing family size coupled with decreasing capacity to earn a living create strong tendencies to modify the relationship after marriage. Families break up or the partners adjust to the situation of deprivation as best they can. The modification of the marital contract can be seen in the varying extent to which the male is marginal to his woman and her children. He may be the purely exploitive pimp or the surprisingly dependable quasi-father. If he is married, he can adhere to the tradition of respectable monogamy or he can attempt to support two or more families, with the inevitable tensions making family life all but unbearable.

The impact upon family life of street life, deprivation, and discrimination, as well as of the reduced capacity to earn a living can be seen in another perspective by considering the basis of the male's status and authority within his family.

MASCULINE AUTHORITY

In contrast to the woman—who even in the ghetto is more closely identified with the home, with kin and the continuity of her family, and with more respectable institutions, such as the church and the school (all of which tend to substantiate an almost unchallengeable respectability about motherhood)—the man in the ghetto derives at least some of his status within many ghetto homes by virtue of his ability to cope with the world of the street and to provide for his family by whatever means become available. The father's "bifocality" is most clearly manifested in the indiscreet free man type of family, such as the Pattersons and the Billits, where the outside activities are manifest. But the most significant manner in which a father becomes a nexus between his family and the street world is shown in the case of the discreet father who gains status in his children's eyes by his coping ability, while not offending them by bringing his "outside" activities into his home. The discreet father, in particular, is able to socialize his sons into deviance.

Socialization into the World of the Street

Fathers socialize their children, particularly their sons, into this street world in a number of ways. The first is by engaging in illegal manipulative strategies such as gambling or pimping. In the case of the Washington family, seven of the boys have records (two on gambling charges) and Arthur Washington has been convicted and jailed for possessing lottery equipment. Both Mr. Washington and Mr. Buchanan gamble, but thus far Andrew Buchanan has not been picked up, nor have any of his sons, who also gamble.

The father's further interest in his son's ability to "make the scene" on the street leads him to be a pal and an instructor in such activities as pool-playing and tavern drinking, which develop the son's sense of what to do with his "idle time" and contribute to his tendency to derive his enjoyment outside of the home.

Fathers provide examples conducive to socialization into the manipulative strategies of the street in other ways also. They give excellent examples of how to lie effectively by the way they handle strangers such as bill collectors, insurance men, various government agents, and social scientists. As Andrew Buchanan candidly admits, "I'm half truthful and I'm half honest." This is not to say that middle-class people do not lie as a manipulative strategy, but rather that deception seems more pervasive and necessary as a survival strategy in the ghetto.

The image that the boy develops of his father as a manipulator of women is fostered by his mother (sometimes intentionally, often inadvertently) through her own suspicion that something is being put over on her. By implication, the cautious and sometimes angry warnings given to her daughters regarding the care they must take in dealing with their boyfriends reverberate upon their conception of their father and makes them suspicious and distrustful of him also. For the boy, on the other hand, this image of the manipulator is something to be copied because it is a central part of how men are expected to behave.

Finally, the father acts as a socializing agent introducing his sons into the manipulative world of the street by his tendency to take pleasure in recalling his exploits as a boy. This is vividly portrayed in the case of Andrew Buchanan who enjoys telling about his wanderings, his living off women, and his introduction to the city and the life of a pimp. Sometimes this recollection takes place as a story volunteered, sometimes it comes about as the result of a son's seeking advice on how to handle his own pressing problems. Thus, Gerald Buchanan receives assurance from his father that he is handling his problems with women "all right" and feels reassured in the rightness of his behavior by his father's statement that he has done all of those things himself.

If the older man is competent to instruct in these coping or survival strategies, he has status and authority in the eyes of younger boys. As soon as a son feels that his "old man" is working game on someone and doing it well, he will listen to what his father has to say, for it is often the most realistic strategy that a ghetto youth can expect to follow.

Domestic Status

While a man undoubtedly has status in the household if he is unemployed, it is commonly recognized that this status is less than if he were employed and bringing in a good paycheck. Andrew Buchanan reflects upon this as he laments his own diminished authority within his household, and Alliena Billit elucidates the wife's point of view when she remarks, "I don't cook for him now that he ain't working."

There are, however, acceptable alternatives to wages. If a man is disabled and this fact is accepted by his family—that is to say, if they recognize that he was once a good provider and that he now does the best he can—he tends to retain his status in the family, as in the case of Lester Frazier. In Stanley Billit's case, however, his wife cannot reconcile herself to his unemployment because of his indiscretions with his disability checks and her feeling that he could be doing something more helpful for her and her children in spite of his disability, which does not, after all, prevent him from working on his car and going out with other women.

A second alternative to adequate wages, besides accepted disability compensations, is part-time work in a job that does not pay an adequate wage to support the family but has a certain prestige. This alternative is really an additional source of prestige over and above that which an accepted disabled man might receive by virtue of his check. There are few such jobs, but with positions in "community organization" and various "training" jobs available through OEO, some men do find them. Only one of the five fathers is presently so employed.

A father's authority is also acknowledged in his household by virtue of his sheer physical power, which enables him to dominate his wife physically if not psychologically. When his brutality is openly expressed, however, it tends to discredit him even in the eyes of his sons (as it did in the case of Edward Patterson) because, as everyone knows, such behavior is a last resort and indicates a basic weakness in familial relationships. A man is supposed to be able to contain his emotions in the family, just as he is expected to play it cool in the street. However, for a man to assure himself and others that he is powerful requires him to use his physical superiority over his wife on occasions and encourages frequent reference to the fact that he is capable of treating women roughly. Boisterous boasting of his ability to handle women roughly is also a part of the image a competent male must present, but again such matters must be handled with discretion, and when they are not, disharmony results. Stanley Billit gives the best example of this behavior.

Because of their frustration in their attempt to be legitimately employed, their constant encounter with their impoverishment, and the generally acknowledged greater respectability and competence of their wives, men have a tendency to resort too often to physical domination of the marital relationship. When this physical power is wisely managed, as in the case of the Washingtons, it contributes to the father's status and authority within the family. When it is not, it can serve as a factor tending to alienate the father from his family, especially his sons, as in the case of Edward Patterson. Some men, such as Andrew Buchanan, are not able to dominate physically because of their disability. This increases their perceived dependency upon their wives, and lowers their status along this dimension within the family.

Complementary to the fact that his wife earns her authority because of her past performance and dependability, a husband can legitimate his authority by being recognized as "respectable." A mother is expected to be so, and her behavior in this area, therefore, does not earn her any extra favor. Since a man is not likely to be so, when he *is*, he increases his status in the eyes of his children, particularly his daughters.

He is an exceptionally good man if he demonstrates his care for his wife and children by not "cutting out" on them. Lester Frazier claims great respect in this regard when he boldly declares, "I ain't got none to speak slack of me," and "If you see me, you see my woman."

An integral part of this respectability is a man's dependability. Again, a woman is expected to care for her children regardless of what happens, but only a *good* man cares for his. On the simplest level, this caring for his children is demonstrated by his willingness to "give to them" when he is able. A father who "turns his pockets out for his kids" is exceptional, one who gives when he can afford it is a good man, and one who gives only sporadically, even though he could give more, is common.

Finally, the father attempts to legitimate his authority within his family by being a pal to his children. He seems to be most effective in this capacity with his young daughters and his older sons. By the time his daughters reach their mid-teens, they are already too basically distrustful of men to be willing to engage in a friendly relationship with their father. He is, perhaps, treated with respect if he is a good man, but the close tie that is often found between father and daughter in the middle class does not seem as prevalent in the ghetto.

Characteristically, he becomes a pal by taking their side in family disputes against the mother's threat of discipline, by giving them small gifts, by going out with them in the case of the older boys, and finally by "understanding" their problems. An interesting pattern characteristic of teenage "outside" girls is that when they themselves become pregnant before marriage they express a desire to go to their biological father (with whom they would have had little to do previously). It is as though this experience creates a deeper understanding between them, in addition to the fact that such an arrangement offers an opportunity for the girl to have her child away from home.

Thus, the father's authority is variously legitimated. (1) It can be legitimated by the father's being an adequate provider or having an accepted excuse for not being one. This income may be by means of legitimate or illegitimate activities, for the distinction has little force, given the ghetto conditions of deprivation. (2) The good man, by virtue of his respectable behavior—as demonstrated by his "giving to" his children and his fidelity to his wife—earns the respect of his family and legitimacy for his authority over his children because they "have nothing over him!" (3) His ability to teach other members of the family "the ropes" is another basis of the ghetto father's authority. The extent to which he can provide his sons with an effective strategy for survival in the manipulative world of the street contributes to his status in their eyes, but detracts from his status in his daughters'. (4) Finally, the ability to be a pal and understand the problems of his children, particularly his older boys, enhances his status in their eyes and validates his authority over them.

All of these elements in a father's role can be seen as offering types of protection against either external threats of economic destitution and social scorn, or internal threats of alienation and distantiation from one's loved ones. The claim to legitimate authority within the household may be made on the basis of one or all of the above, but characteristically the type of claim is related to the degree of the father's marginality to his family.

Masculine Authority and Marginality

If this typology of marginality is now examined in the context of the method of legitimating the father's (or father substitute's) authority within the household, the following relationships are suggested:

1. The traditional monogamous father tends to legitimate his authority on the basis of two more or less equal aspects of his relationship to the external world; that is, (a) his ability to be an adequate provider, or the fact that his inability is understood as the result of a justified disability, and (b) his ability to claim that he is respectable. He is affectionate toward his wife and children, of course. But he tends to be, at least verbally, an advocate of the patriarchal type of family. He is generally not an adaptive strategist because he has been able more or less to make it by legitimate means and because his principles prohibit him from being one.

2. The "discreetly free father," on the other hand, tends to legitimate his authority within the household on the basis of his being a warm loving pal to his children and an expressive companion to a more instrumentally oriented wife. He tends also to be able to muster respect for his ability to cope with the environment by means of manipulative strategies such as gambling, working game on friends, and discreet affairs with other women, which provide him with victories his sons in particular would like to emulate. He is or was an adequate provider, and his present disability is understood by his family. He expresses concern for "skeletons" in the family's closet,

indicating that he would like to draw upon past respectable behavior in the disciplining of his children, but cannot.

3. The indiscreet father has least control over his children because he has little to justify his authority. If he is able to provide for his family, his status is still marred by his split in allegiance. If he is unable, his disability is not accepted and he must prefabricate an instrumental role in order to protect himself in this vulnerable area. (Thus Mr. Billit, though unemployed, thinks of himself as having an earning power of $150 a week, the amount, with overtime, that he made when he was employed.) If he is not able to provide for his family, he develops an ability to cope with the world of the street, but otherwise he will largely ignore the street world. He generally has little justification for his authority on the basis of his expressive ability, and none as a model for traditional respectable behavior.

4. The situation of the boyfriend is simplified since only two of the four types are really concerned with the children at all. The quasi-father seems to be inclined to legitimate his authority on the basis of his instrumental effectiveness and coping ability. The supportive biological father, on the other hand, stresses his affective role, while at the same time offering support to the family. He, more so than the quasi-father, wants the children to think of him as a "good guy," perhaps because he has a greater stake in their affection since they are biologically his. In the case of the quasi-father, where the obligation is not as apparent—but is nevertheless present—the fact of support can be called upon as a legitimate reason for assuming some authority over the family.

Thus, the father in project families is not simply subordinate to his wife, as the term "matrifocal" might imply. His status depends not only upon his capacity to earn a living and his further willingness to share that living with his family, but also upon his degree of adherence to the norms of respectability, his ability to cope with the harsh realities of the ghetto, and his capacity to be a "pal" to his children. The family that seems best able to survive as a family unit in a situation where there is little hope of upward mobility or of sufficient income from legitimate sources is, as we might expect, the family that is best able to cope with its environment as it presents itself. In such a family, the father is typically the discreet free man. His ability to effectively manage two worlds is in large measure responsible for the fact that his family retains cohesiveness in spite of being open to the disintegrating influences of street life.

The Constant Threat to Authority

What is characteristic of the ghetto home, however, is the fact that children constantly question the right of the parents to govern them, and parents seem unable to firmly establish this authority in response to such questioning. Children know that their parents (particularly their father) are unable to adequately protect them from the harsh realities of their world and are largely unable to offer them reliable information or dependable role models to enable them to better themselves in the world outside the ghetto. When parents attempt to guide their children along more respectable lines of behavior, they are quite frequently reminded, "You do the same things you tell us not to do. Why can't we do them?" Parents thus watch their children's development with mixed sorrow and a peculiar pride in the fact that their children are following after them, even though they know that the road leads nowhere.

Finally, parents are confronted quite straightforwardly with the fact that they need their children's love. Boys, in particular, threaten to withhold this by running away from home to live with a relative more likely to grant them what they want in terms of the small pleasures of life. Girls, such as Geraldine and Annie Lou, who have been "farmed out," will hold this against their parents and taunt them by saying that they liked living where they were sent better than living at home.

The result is a constant threat of insurrection in the home. Parents often try to cope with this by letting a child have his way and intervening in his life only in extreme situations, often after it is too late to prevent him from being labeled as a delinquent, a sexual deviant, or a lush. Such belated intervention only further weakens the bargaining power of the parents and submits their authority to further questioning.

Because parental authority is constantly being subverted, a common recourse is to call upon recognized authority outside the family. Neighbors will not do, both because they are involved in the same struggle themselves, and because they are normally unwilling to intervene in another family's domestic squabbles—unless it is to defend their own child from presumed attack. The police, therefore, are quite often called upon to settle domestic troubles between parents themselves and between parents and their children. Such intervention is both needed and hated, since it makes it obvious that the family is unable to govern its own life. Furthermore, persons who thus intervene are very likely to acquire a closer relationship with one member of the family—ordinarily the wife—and incur the wrath of another—usually the husband. Outside intervention thus restores order in the household without solving or resolving any of the problems that precipitated the disorder. At the same time, such intervention heightens suspicion among family members and churns resentments likely to erupt later into further discord. Such discord tends to increase the father's marginality and desire to desert.

Project families thus achieve their cohesiveness in the midst of many forces, both internal and external, that threaten their very existence. They respond to these threats in many ways, producing a variety of family life styles. The marginality of the father or his surrogate is one way of looking at some of this variety. Until the lower-class Negro man's status has been greatly improved in the world outside the ghetto through better training, better education, and above all, better jobs, it does not seem likely that men in the project will be able to assume a more central role in the life of their families, nor that they will desist in training their sons in the only techniques of survival that seem to work in their experience—even though these techniques of survival have a tendency to be detrimental to their family and to perpetuate its problems.

A Policy Postscript

Although it is true that the incidence of poverty in America has been decreasing in a generally expanding economy, the benefits of this prosperity have not been shared equally by all portions of our population. Despite the war on poverty and the passage of several civil rights bills, poverty is still a problem for the black American to a greater extent than it is for the white. Although Negro Americans constitute only about a tenth of our population, they comprise about a fifth of the poor population. Almost half of all black Americans are poor, and in some respects their situation is worsening. According to recent Labor Department statistics, you were about three times as likely to be poor if you were black in 1959. In 1966 this ratio increased to three-and-one-half to one. A mid-decade census further revealed that in eight out of twelve cities where surveys were made, residential segregation *increased* over the period 1959–1965, and the conditions within the ghetto continued to deteriorate.[1] Since 1960 black Americans have become more urbanized than white, and now over 75 per cent live in urban areas. In the cities they have not found the promised land. They have found instead overcrowded, rat-infested streets, a scarcity of good jobs for which they can qualify, and an apparently indifferent white America basking in suburban seclusion.

Why is poverty more apparent in black America than in white? Currently, there are two basic approaches to this question. One places more emphasis upon factors exterior to the black community; the other focuses upon factors within it.

It used to be that such a question was not raised at all since it was unthinkable that a Negro could be expected to live like any other

[1] United States Department of Labor, Report No. 332, "Social and Economic Conditions of Negroes in the United States," *Current Population Reports,* Series P–23, No. 24 (October 1967), p. xi.

American. However, with the passing of biological racism and the doctrine of the inherent inferiority of black Americans, prejudice has not ended. Prejudice and discrimination still exact a heavy price from black Americans. Herman Miller estimates, for example, that in 1961 alone discrimination cost black Americans sixteen billion dollars.[2] The accusation of the Kerner Commission that "white racism" was the most significant cause of the riots suggests further that all of the legislation since the Brown decision of 1954 has done little to relieve the basic frustrations of the ghetto. Discrimination is undoubtedly a factor contributing to black impoverishment. But precisely how does it operate, how much of a factor is it, and how can it be overcome?

On the other hand, the answers that focus on factors within the black community have tended to concentrate on the structure of black families—particularly since the 1965 release of *The Negro Family: The Case for National Action.* In this report the then Undersecretary of Labor, Daniel Patrick Moynihan, called attention to the possible role of the family in perpetuating poverty intergenerationally. He called the problems arising out of the lower-class Negro family a "tangle of pathology."[3] Those reading the report tended to assume that he was drawing attention away from basic economic reforms and providing further material for the white racists by dwelling upon illegitimacy rates, incidence of broken homes, trends in welfare payments, and the extent to which these could be seen to contribute to intergenerational poverty. "The present tangle of pathology is capable of perpetuating itself without assistance from the white world," Moynihan wrote. "The cycle can be broken only if these distortions are set right. In a word, a national effort toward the problems of Negro America must be directed toward the question of family structure."[4]

Even though no specific policy was proposed for meeting the problems of the lower-class Negro family, the emphasis upon "family

[2] Herman Miller, "The Dimensions of Poverty" in *Poverty as a Public Issue,* ed. Ben B. Seligman (New York: The Free Press, 1965), p. 32.

[3] The United States Department of Labor, Office of Planning and Research, *The Negro Family: The Case for National Action* (Washington, D.C.: The United States Government Printing Office, 1965), p. 47.

[4] Charles V. Willie, "Intergenerational Poverty" (Paper presented at The Pennsylvania State University, June 5, 1968), p. 2. For another critique of the Moynihan Report, see Andrew Billingsley, *Black Families in White America* (Englewood Cliffs, N.J.: Prentice-Hall, Inc., 1968), pp. 199–204.

structure" has led many to assume that Moynihan favors treating family pathologies *before* basic economic reform. As Charles Willie sees the Moynihan thesis, it constitutes one of two prominent ideologies. It "asserts that the presence or absence of poverty either is a function of strengths or deficiencies in the person, family and clan (or ethnic group)." The opposing ideology asserts that poverty is "a function of strengths or deficiencies in institutional arrangement and the opportunity system of the total community." [5]

A third response to the question of black poverty does not concern itself primarily with the question of why black poverty is more prevalent than white. It sees the problem as one of *American* poverty in the midst of affluence, and points to a basic failure in the distributive system which demands basic alterations. This position reasons that if the economic aspects of poverty were eliminated through some form of guaranteed annual income, the problems of the ghetto would be much easier to deal with, even if they did not disappear altogether.

Does poverty then derive mainly from interpersonal problems or institutional ones? Do you try first to change the individual and his style of life, or do you attempt to change the system that sustains—or restrains—that style of life? These are pertinent policy questions for which the socio-psychological answers are not in agreement. Willie notes, "Probably there is an interaction effect between these two 'explanations' of poverty. Research is needed to determine the relative contribution, if any, of forces external or internal to particular populations to the perpetuation of poverty among nearly one fifth of the people in this nation." [6] Willie goes on to suggest that failure in family structure and function might better predict the incidence of poverty among white populations than black because the latter have the additional burden of racial discrimination to overcome. The effect of family structure on the intergenerational transmission of poverty cannot fairly be assessed in the black population until this discrimination is eliminated.

> Because whites, in general, have had free access to the opportunities produced by institutional change, the residual number of poor people in this racial category very well might be a function

[5] *Ibid.*
[6] *Ibid.*

> more of personal and family connected deficiencies. It is not concluded that poverty among whites cannot be further reduced by more change in the institutional system of society. Rather, it is suggested that new manipulations of social institutions probably will net a smaller rate of change in the proportion of poor whites as compared with poor non-whites, since most whites who could benefit from the major institutional changes have already taken advantage of them.[7]

At the center of the attempt to draw policy from social science research is the concept of culture. The term "culture" ordinarily is used to mean "all that which is non-biological and socially transmitted, including artistic, social, ideological and religious patterns of behavior, and the techniques for mastering the environment." [8] In short, culture is patterned and learned behavior together with its artifacts. The term is used axiomatically in social science in that it declares that human interaction is orderly—that is to say patterned—and, therefore, susceptible to scientific investigation and generalization.

There is, however, a further problem when the term "culture" is utilized in the phrase "culture of poverty." Here it is ordinarily conceived of as a way of life that is significantly different from the core culture (the non-impoverished culture), and as such is more properly referred to as a subculture. The relationship of this subculture to the core culture has been variously described in the literature.[9]

The pertinent questions from a policy viewpoint are, "Is there in fact a culture of poverty? If there is, is it in any important sense a 'cause' of poverty? If it is a cause, how susceptible to change is it and by what means can it be ethically and most efficiently changed to minimize or eliminate its tendency to perpetuate poverty?" Many of the current studies on the culture of poverty are directed largely toward answering the first question—or raising doubts about the existence of a culture of poverty.[10] The second question regarding its causative role

[7] *Ibid.*, p. 10.

[8] Charles Winick, *A Dictionary of Anthropology* (New York: Philosophical Library, 1956), p. 144.

[9] For a good discussion of the various descriptions, see Jack L. Roach and Orville R. Gursslin, "An Evaluation of the Concept 'Culture of Poverty,'" *Social Forces*, XLV, No. 3 (March 1967), pp. 383–92.

[10] A few of the advocates of the culture of poverty concept are: Oscar Lewis, *La Vida* (New York: Random House, Inc., 1965); Michael Harrington, *The*

is generally assumed by definition.[11] The last questions are, it would seem, answered not so much on the basis of scientific findings—since the role of the culture of poverty in the perpetuation of poverty has not yet been adequately explained—as on the basis of ideological commitments. In most instances, it would seem, the ethics arise out of a compassionate humanism.

This study supports the contention that there *is* a culture of poverty —a distinctive style of life that is shared and is apparently similar in black ghettoes all over America.[12] This study also supports, though less strongly, the contention that such a culture does contribute to the perpetuation of poverty by compounding the problems of control over children and spouses and supporting a style of life that is rewarding within the ghetto ("living sweet," for example) but detrimental to mobility out of the ghetto. No answers to the last questions are derivable directly from this study. Ironically, such answers will come, most probably, out of attempts to eliminate poverty. Policy decisions will, thus, most likely *precede* precise answers to these questions.

As Lee Rainwater sees it, the existence of a culture of poverty argues for radical alteration in the conditions of isolation and deprivation which are the basic and distinctive conditions to which the poor must adapt. The culture of poverty enables them to survive in their harsh restricted economic and physical environment. Do away with the basic economic injustice insofar as it is possible to do this, and the odds are that a style of life more closely resembling that of the core culture will emerge because there is no longer any need to adapt to isolation and

---

Other America (Baltimore: Penguin Books, 1963); and Lee Rainwater, "Marital Sexuality in Three Cultures of Poverty," *Journal of Marriage and the Family,* XXVI (November 1964), 457–66. Critics are represented by Roach and Gursslin, *op. cit.;* Hylan Lewis, "Child Rearing Among Low Income Families" (Washington, D.C.: The Washington Center for Metropolitan Studies, 1961); and Willie, *op. cit.*

[11] See particularly the discussion in Roach and Gursslin, *op. cit.*, pp. 38 ff.

[12] Similar styles of life have been recorded in Elliot Liebow, *Tally's Corner* (Boston: Little, Brown & Company, 1967); Hylan Lewis, *Blackways of Kent* (Chapel Hill: University of North Carolina Press, 1961); Sinclair Drake and Horace Cayton, *Black Metropolis* (New York: Harcourt, Brace & World, Inc., 1945); E. Franklin Frazier, *The Negro Family in the United States* (Chicago: The University of Chicago Press, 1961); and Allison Davis and John Dollard, *Children of Bondage* (Washington, D.C.: The American Council on Higher Education, 1940).

deprivation. After all, as Andrew Buchanan put it, "Don't ask me why I eat chittlins, I eat chittlins because I can't afford a steak."

Project dwellers do not have a separate system of ultimate values. They want very much to be able to live like the average American. However, because they cannot and because it is painful to continue to evaluate oneself by norms that are unattainable, they have accepted an alternate set of norms that enables them to maintain some sense of self-esteem in the midst of their isolation and deprivation. Chittlins are now a significant part of what is called "soul food" in a further attempt to make desirable what is most readily attainable and to provide a concrete sacrament bestowing identity within a black brotherhood.

Some form of income maintenance that goes beyond providing a minimum subsistance level of living for poor Americans seems, in light of what we now know about the problems of the poor, to be the most just (and in the long run, the most likely) means of eliminating poverty and, along with it, its culture. It should be further obvious, however, that if the black American is to benefit equally from such reforms, racial discrimination must cease, and that even with an income maintenance program some families will need special help. Income maintenance should be considered the major strategy against poverty, but not the only one.

The most acceptable form of such a program—both to the poor and to the average American—is one that ties income as closely as possible to a job. The majority of project dwellers would rather work than receive a dole and, in fact, the majority of the poor do work and still remain in poverty.[13] A tight labor market plus a wage supplement program would by themselves thus largely do away with poverty in America.[14]

[13] According to the U.S. Bureau of the Census, *Current Population Reports*, Series P–20, No. 54, "The Extent of Poverty in the United States: 1959–1966" (Washington, D.C.: The United States Government Printing Office), p. 30, thirty-one per cent of all families below the poverty level worked full-time in 1966, 27.2 per cent worked part of the year, and 1.2 per cent were in the Armed Forces. Among non-white families the percentage that worked and still remained in poverty was somewhat higher: 36.4 per cent worked a full year, 30.7 per cent worked part of the year, 0.6 per cent were in the Armed Forces, and 32.3 per cent did not work.

[14] A good summary statement of a wage supplement program is provided by Paul S. Anderson, *The Washington Post,* May 26, 1968, p. 5. It is an adaptation from a forthcoming book by Mr. Anderson, *Economic Policies for Efficiency,*

There will always be those who cannot work, whether because of age or mental, physical, or sociological handicaps. In justice, these should receive the same supports through other forms of income maintenance. Finally, there might be a residue of those who are apparently able but unwilling to work—the "leaches" the average American fears will benefit unjustly from any blanket program of income maintenance. What about these persons? In all probability, their numbers will be small.[15] It is further not likely that they will be discernible *in advance* of the implementation of any broad program to eliminate poverty.

The moral question that must then be weighed is, "Should we continue to punish the vast majority of the poor because we fear that a few will benefit unjustly?" The time has come when the affirmative answer to such a question can no longer be accepted. American cities are in crisis, the need is pressing to rebuild the American dream concretely in cities once more fit for human habitation. The economic and technological resources necessary to meet the poverty problem head-on are at hand. This problem must not be evaded any longer.

Justice and Welfare. He proposes a program that would bring wages up to $1.50 an hour (if the target level income is to be $3,000), the wage supplement to be given on the actual number of hours worked. The net cost of the plan would be, he estimates, $10–12 billion a year.

Lee Rainwater proposes that we aim much higher and bring the low level income into the median income range, thus bringing about a nation of average men (as far as income goes) over a ten-year period. In 1965 that would have meant that 60 per cent of the population would have fallen within the $7,000 and $7,999 per year bracket. In terms of 1965 dollars, this would mean a minimum wage of $2.95 per hour. No total cost figures are provided. Lee Rainwater, "Toward a Nation of Average Men, Income Equalization in a Just Society" (Paper prepared for the UDA Airlie House Conference, October 7–9, 1966, forthcoming).

[15] Data on the actual amount of "welfare chiseling," for example, indicate that a maximum of 7.4 per cent of the recipients on ADC in any given state *could* be guilty of "intentionally concealing or misrepresenting the facts" with regard to their welfare eligibility. In all probability, the average was much closer to 2.5 per cent. See "Eligibility of Families Receiving Aid to Families with Dependent Children" (Washington, D.C.: Department of Health, Education and Welfare, July, 1963). Quoted in David Matza, "Poverty and Disrepute," *Contemporary Social Problems,* eds. Merton and Nesbit (New York: Harcourt, Brace & World, Inc., 1961).

Bibliography

Abrahams, Roger D. "Playing the Dozens," *Journal of American Folklore,* LXXV (July 1962), 209–20.

Bacon, Margaret, I. L. Child, and H. Barry, III. "A Cross-Cultural Study of Correlates of Crime," *Journal of Abnormal and Social Psychology,* LXVI (March 1963), 291–300.

Barber, Bernard. "Family Status, Local Community Status, and Social Stratification," *Pacific Sociological Review,* XIV (Spring, 1961), 3–10.

Becker, Howard. *The Outsiders: Studies in the Sociology of Deviance.* New York: The Macmillan Company, 1966.

Bernard, Jessie. "Marital Stability and Patterns of Status Variables," *Journal of Marriage and the Family,* XXVIII (November 1966), 421–45.

———. *Marriage and Family Among Negroes.* Englewood Cliffs, N.J.: Prentice-Hall, Inc., 1966.

———. "The State of the Knowledge." Paper prepared for the Ohio Wesleyan Conference on Race, 1965.

Billingsley, Andrew. *Black Families in White America.* Englewood Cliffs, N.J.: Prentice-Hall, Inc., 1968.

Bott, Elizabeth. *Family and Social Network: Roles, Norms and External Relationships in Ordinary Urban Families.* London: Tavistock Publications, 1957.

Bruyn, Severyn T. *The Human Perspective in Sociology: The Methodology of Participant Observation.* Englewood Cliffs, N.J.: Prentice-Hall, Inc., 1966.

Clark, Kenneth. *Dark Ghetto.* New York: Harper & Row, Publishers, 1965.

———. *Youth in the Ghetto: A Study of the Consequences of Powerlessness.* New York: Harlem Youth Opportunities Unlimited, Inc., 1964.

Cohen, Albert K. "Social Disorganization and Deviant Behavior," in *Sociology Today, ed.* Robert Merton, *et al.* New York: Harper & Row, Publishers, 1965.

D'Andrade, R. G. "Father Absence and Cross-Sex Identification." Unpublished Doctoral Dissertation, Harvard University, 1962.

Davis, Allison, and John Dollard. *Children of Bondage*. Washington, D.C.: American Council on Higher Education, 1940.

DeCoy, Robert H. *The Nigger Bible*. Los Angeles: Holloway House Publishing Company, 1967.

Dollard, John. *Caste and Class in a Southern Town*. Second Edition. New Haven: Yale University Press, 1939.

———. "The Dozens: The Dialect of Insult," *American Imago*, I (1939), 3–24.

Drake, Sinclair, and Horace Cayton. *Black Metropolis*. New York: Harcourt, Brace & World, Inc., 1945.

Dworkin, Barry, and Susan Dworkin. "Cool: Young Adults in the Ghetto." Columbia, Mo.: University of Missouri, n.d. (mimeographed).

Erikson, Erik H. "The Concept of Identity in Race Relations: Notes and Queries," *Daedalus*, XCV (Winter, 1966), 145–71.

———. "Growth and the Crises of the 'Healthy Personality,' " in *Personality in Nature, Society and Culture*, ed. Clyde Kluckholm, *et al*. New York: Alfred A. Knopf, Inc., 1967.

Fisher, Ann, *et al*. "The Occurrence of the Extended Family at the Origin of the Family of Procreation: A Developmental Approach to Negro Family Structure." Paper presented to the American Anthropological Association, Denver, November, 1965.

Frazier, E. Franklin. *The Negro Family in the United States*. Chicago: University of Chicago Press, 1960.

———. *Black Bourgeoisie: The Rise of a New Middle Class*. New York: The Free Press, 1957.

Gans, Herbert. "The Negro Family: Reflections on the Moynihan Report," *Commonweal*, LXXXIII (October 1965), 47–51.

Glazer, Nathan. "Foreword" to *The Negro Family in the United States* by E. Franklin Frazier. Chicago: University of Chicago Press, 1960.

Glueck, Stanley, and Eleanor Glueck. *Unraveling Juvenile Delinjuency*. New York: Commonweal Fund, 1960.

Goody, Jack. *The Developmental Cycle in Domestic Groups*. Cambridge, England: Cambridge Papers in Social Anthropology, No. 1, 1958.

Griffin, John H. *Black Like Me*. Boston: Houghton Mifflin Company, 1961.

Habenstien, Robert W., and Allan D. Coult. "The Function of Extended Kinship in Urban Society," Kansas City: A Final Progress Report of Community Studies, Inc., 1965 (mimeographed).

Haley, Jay. "Family Experiments: A New Type of Experimentation," in *The Psychosocial Interiors of the Family: A Sourcebook for the Study of Whole Families,* ed. Gerald Handel. Chicago: Aldine Publishing Company, 1967.

Hammond, Boone. "The Contest System: A Survival Technique." St. Louis: Washington University Essay Series in Sociology, December 1965 (mimeographed).

Handel, Gerald. "The Psychological Study of Whole Families." Chicago: Social Research, Inc., n.d. (mimeographed).

Harrington, Michael. *The Other America.* Baltimore: Penguin Books, 1963.

Hess, Robert D., and Gerald Handel. *Family Worlds.* Chicago: University of Chicago Press, 1959.

Horton, John. "Time and Colored People," *Trans-action,* IV (April 1967), 5–12.

Kardiner, Abram, and Lionel Ovesey. *The Mark of Oppression.* New York: Meridian Books, 1962.

Kohn, M. L., and J. A. Clausen. "Parental Authority Behavior and Schizophrenia," *American Journal of Orthopsychiatry,* XXVI (1956), 297–313.

Kriesberg, Louis, and Seymour Bellin. "Fatherless Families and Housing: A Study of Dependency, Final Report." New York: Syracuse Youth Development Center, 1966 (mimeographed).

Lampman, Robert. "The Low Income Population and Economic Growth," Study Paper No. 12. Washington, D.C.: United States Congress Joint Economic Committee, 1959.

Lefcowitz, Myron J. "Poverty and Negro-White Family Structure." Washington, D.C.: Agenda Paper for White House Planning Session on Race, November 1965 (mimeographed).

Leichter, Jope Jensen, and William E. Mitchell. *Kinship and Casework.* New York: Russell Sage Foundation, 1967.

Lerman, Paul. "Argot, Symbolic Deviance and Subculture Delinquency." *American Sociological Review,* XXXII (April 1967), 209–24.

Lewis, Hylan. *Blackways of Kent.* Chapel Hill: University of North Carolina Press, 1961.

———. "The Family: Resources for Change." Washington, D.C.: Agenda Paper V, White House Planning Session on Race, November 1965 (mimeographed).

Lewis, Oscar. "An Anthropological Approach to Family Studies," *American Journal of Sociology,* LV (March 1950), 460–75.

———. *Five Families.* New York: Science Editions, Inc., 1962.

———. *The Children of Sanchez.* New York: Random House, Inc., 1961.

———. *La Vida.* New York: Random House, Inc., 1965.

Liebow, Elliot. *Tally's Corner.* Boston: Little, Brown & Company, 1967.

McClelland, David. *The Achieving Society.* Princeton, New Jersey: D. Van Nostrand Co., Inc., 1961.

Matza, David. "Poverty and Disrepute," in *Contemporary Social Problems,* eds. Robert Merton and Robert Nesbit. New York: Harcourt, Brace & World, Inc., 1966.

Miller, Herman. "The Dimensions of Poverty," in *Poverty as a Public Issue,* ed. Ben B. Seligman. New York: The Free Press, 1965.

———. "Trends in the Income of Families and Persons in the United States, 1947–1960." Washington, D.C.: United States Department of Commerce, Bureau of the Census, 1960.

Miller, W. B. "Lower-Class Culture as a Generating Milieu of Gang Delinquency," *Journal of Social Issues,* XIV (1958), 5–19.

Mischel, Walter. "Delay of Gratification, Need for Achievement and Acquiescence in Another Culture," *Journal of Abnormal and Social Psychology,* LXXII (May 1961), 543–52.

———. "Father Absence and Delay of Gratification," *Journal of Abnormal Psychology,* LXXIII (February 1962), 116–24.

Moore, William. "A Portrait: The Culturally Disadvantaged Pre-School Negro Child." Unpublished Doctoral Dissertation, St. Louis University, 1964.

Mowrer, O., and A. D. Ullman. "Time as a Determinant in Integrative Learning," *Psychological Review,* LXXII (1965), 61–90.

Moynihan, Daniel P. "A Family Policy for the Nation," *America,* CXIII (September 1965), 280–83.

———. "Employment, Income, and the Ordeal of the Negro Family," *Daedalus,* XCIV (Fall, 1965), 745–70.

———. "A Review of the Negro Family in the United States," *Commonweal,* LXXXIII (October 1966), 47–51.

Parsons, Talcott. "The Kinship System of the United States," *The American Anthropologist,* XLV (January 1943), 22–38.

———, and Robert Bales. *Family Socialization and Interaction Process.* New York: The Free Press, 1955.

Pettigrew, Thomas F. *A Profile of the Negro American.* Princeton, New Jersey: D. Van Nostrand Co., Inc., 1964.

Rainwater, Lee. "Marital Stability and Patterns of Status Variables: A Comment," *Journal of Marriage and the Family,* XXVIII (November 1966), 442–45.

———. *And the Poor Get Children.* Chicago: Quadrangle Books, 1960.

———, and William L. Yancey. *The Moynihan Report and the Politics of Controversy.* Cambridge, Mass.: The M.I.T. Press, 1967.

———. "Poverty and Deprivation in the Crisis of the American City." Washington, D.C.: A Statement presented to the United States Senate Committee on Government Operations, Subcommittee on Executive Reorganization, December 1966 (mimeographed).

———. "Toward a Nation of Average Men: Income Equalization and a Just Society." Paper prepared for publication based on the UDA Airlie House Conference, October 1966 (mimeographed).

———. "The Problem of Lower Class Culture and the Poverty War Strategy." St Louis: Washington University, Social Science Institute, Occasional Paper Number 34, 1967 (mimeographed).

———. "Work and Identity in the Lower Class," *Planning for a Nation of Cities,* ed. Sam H. Warner. Cambridge, Mass.: M.I.T. Press, 1967.

Reise, Hertha. *Heal the Hurt Child.* Chicago: University of Chicago Press, 1962.

Reiss, Ira. "Teenage Sexual Codes," *The Annals of the American Academy of Political and Social Science,* CCXXXVIII (November 1961), 53–62.

Roach, Jack L., and Orville R. Gursslin. "An Evaluation of the Concept 'Culture of Poverty,'" *Social Forces,* XLV, No. 3 (March, 1967), 383–92.

Ryan, William. "The Negro Family ('The Moynihan Report')." Boston, 1965 (mimeographed).

Sawyer, Ethel. "A Study of a Public Lesbian Community." St. Louis: Washington University Essay Series in Sociology, 1965 (mimeographed).

Schulz, David A. "Some Aspects of the Policeman's Role as It Impinges Upon the Lower-Class Negro Family." Paper presented to the American Sociological Association, Boston, August 1968 (mimeographed).

———. "Variations in Complete and Incomplete Families of the Negro Lower Class." Unpublished Doctoral Dissertation, Washington University, 1968 (mimeographed).

Shostak, Arthur. "The Poverty of Welfare in America," in *New Perspective on Poverty,* eds. Arthur B. Shostak and William Gomberg. Englewood Cliffs, N.J.: Prentice-Hall, Inc., 1965.

Strauss, Anselm, and Barney Glazer. "Discovery of Substantive Theory: A Basic Strategy Underlying Qualitative Research," *American Behavioral Scientist,* VIII (February 1965), 5–12.

Stromberg, Jerome. "Perspectives on Pathology, Socialization, Religion, and World View of (Project) Residents." St. Louis: Internal Working Paper Number Five, The Social Science Institute of Washington University, 1966 (mimeographed).

———. "A Preliminary Report on Housing and Community Experiences of (Project) Residents." St. Louis: Washington University, Social Science Institute, Occasional Paper Number 1, 1966 (mimeographed.)

Udry, Richard J. "Marital Instability by Race, Sex, Education and Occupation Using 1960 Census Data," *American Journal of Sociology*, LXXII (September 1966), 203–6.

United States Department of Commerce, Bureau of the Census. "The Extent of Poverty in the United States: 1959–1966." *Current Populations Reports.* Washington, D.C.: United States Government Printing Office, Series P-20, No. 54, May 31, 1968.

———. "Household and Family Characteristics, March 1966," *Population Characteristics.* Washington, D.C.: United States Government Printing Office, Series P-20, No. 164, April 12, 1967.

———. "Negro Population, March 1965," *Population Characteristics.* Washington, D.C.: United States Government Printing Office, Series, P-20, No. 155, September 27, 1966.

United States Department of Labor. "Social and Economic Conditions of Negroes in the United States," *Current Population Reports.* Washington, D.C.: United States Government Printing Office, Series P-23, No. 24, October 1967.

———. Office of Planning and Research. *The Negro Family: The Case for National Action.* Washington, D.C.: United States Government Printing Office, 1965.

United States Social Security Administration. "Counting the Poor," *Social Security Bulletin,* XXVIII. Washington, D.C.: The United States Government Printing Office, January 1965.

Willie, Charles V. "Intergenerational Poverty." Paper presented at The Pennsylvania State University, June 5, 1968 (mimeographed).

Winick, Charles. *A Dictionary of Anthropology.* New York: Philosophical Library, 1956.

Yancey, William, and Boone Hammond. "Glossary of Negro Jive." St. Louis: Washington University, Social Science Institute, 1965 (mimeographed).

Index